THE
EXILIC AGE

THE
EXILIC AGE

by

CHARLES FRANCIS WHITLEY
M.A., B.A., PH.D

Philadelphia
THE WESTMINSTER PRESS

First published in Great Britain in 1957
by Longmans, Green & Co., Ltd.

Library of Congress Catalog Card No.: 58–5127

Printed in Great Britain

PREFACE

THE sixth century B.C. was an age of decline and develop ment. The ancient civilisations of Egypt and Babylonia had run their courses, while the Indo-European mind was beginning to make significant intellectual advances. It was in this century of change that the Jews were carried into exile in Babylon, where their religious beliefs were subjected to the most critical tests. An attempt is therefore made in the following pages to outline the historical and intellectual movements of the age and to interpret the work of Jeremiah, Ezekiel, and Deutero-Isaiah in relation to such movements. Apart from preliminary questions of date and authorship the discussion of these prophets is concerned with their contribution to Hebrew religious thought in this re-markable period of history. As far as possible they have been allowed to speak for themselves, and quotations are taken from the Revised Standard Version as well as from the Revised Version.

I should like to acknowledge here my debt to the Rev. C. A. Simpson, D.D., Regius Professor of Hebrew and Canon of Christ Church, Oxford, not only for stimulating discussions on the subject but also for reading the manuscript and offering much constructive criticism. The Rev. Dr. C. R. North, Emeritus Professor of Hebrew, University College of North Wales, Bangor, also kindly read the typescript and made valuable suggestions.

C. F. WHITLEY

CONTENTS

ABBREVIATIONS

A.H.R.	*American Historical Review.*
A.J.S.L.	*American Journal of Semitic Languages and Literature.*
A.N.E.T.	*Ancient Near Eastern Texts Relating to the Old Testament,* edited by J. B. Pritchard (Princeton, 2nd edn. 1955).
A.R.A.B.	*Ancient Records of Assyria and Babylonia,* by D. D. Luckenbill, 2 vols., 1926–27.
A.T.R.	*Anglican Theological Review.*
B.A.	*The Biblical Archaeologist.*
B.A.S.O.R.	*Bulletin of the American Schools of Oriental Research.*
B.D.B.	*A Hebrew and English Lexicon of the Old Testament,* by Brown, Driver, and Briggs (corrected impression 1952), Oxford.
B.J.R.L.	*Bulletin of the John Rylands Library.*
C.A.H.	*Cambridge Ancient History.*
E.B.	*Encyclopaedia Biblica.*
E.T.	*Expository Times.*
F.u.F.	*Forschungen und Fortschritte.*
H.A.T.	*Handbuch zum Alten Testament.*
H.D.B.	*Hastings' Dictionary of the Bible.*
H.T.R.	*Harvard Theological Review.*
H.U.C.A.	*Hebrew Union College Annual.*
I.C.C.	*International Critical Commentary.*
J.B.L.	*Journal of Biblical Literature.*
J.E.A.	*Journal of Egyptian Archaeology.*
J.N.E.S.	*Journal of Near Eastern Studies.*
J.T.S.	*Journal of Theological Studies.*
LXX	The Septuagint.
M.T.	Massoretic Text.
P.E.F.Q.S.	Quarterly Statement of the Palestine Exploration Fund.
R.A.	*Revue d'Assyriologie et d'Archéologie orientale.*
R.B.	*Revue Biblique.*
R.S.V.	Revised Standard Version.
T.R.	*Theologische Rundschau.*
V.T.	*Vetus Testamentum.*
Z.A.W.	*Zeitschrift für die alttestamentliche Wissenschaft.*

I

HISTORY AND THE EXILIC AGE

HISTORY, said Gibbon, is 'little more than the register of the crimes, follies, and misfortunes of mankind'.[1] Yet despite such a lamentable estimate of humanity we can also discern in its records some actions of men and some movements of thought which were destined to have an enduring place in civilisation. From evidence available to us today we can study man's long conflict with nature and his conquests in the material realm until in the middle of the first millennium B.C. we observe the emergence of certain concepts which are of epoch-making importance in the history of the intellectual and religious developments of mankind. Of course, from the eighth century onwards religious movements were becoming evident throughout the Orient. Commenting on the rise of historical religions G. F. Moore wrote: 'The great religions of this class have their beginnings in the centuries from the eighth to the fifth centuries before the Christian era. This is the age of Taoism in China; of the Upanishads, of Buddhism, and of the precursors of Hinduism in India; of Zoroaster in Iran; of the Orphic-Pythagorean movement in Greece; and of the Hebrew prophets.'[2] The most significant movements of these centuries fall, however, within the period of the Jewish exile in Babylon. For apart from this being specifically the age of Jeremiah, Ezekiel, and Deutero-Isaiah it was in other respects an age of profound religious and philosophical thought as well as of far-reaching historical developments. Hence it becomes evident that any profitable study of the message of these prophets

[1] *Decline and Fall of the Roman Empire*, chap. 3, 2.
[2] *History of Religions*, vol. I, 1914, p. viii; cf. also George Galloway, *The Philosophy of Religion*, 1914, p. 133.

cannot afford to overlook this wider background of thought and history. Indeed S. A. Cook not only regarded this as a time 'when a new Palestine was taking shape' but was also of the opinion that biblical 'discussions of today go back essentially to the Exilic Age of about twenty-five centuries ago'.[1] More recently Professor Herbert Butterfield in his book *Christianity and History* remarked that 'the events in the centre of which stands the famous Exile of the ancient Jews ought to be an element in the curriculum of every serious student of the past'.[2]

While most Old Testament scholars would recognise this period as one of widespread religious movements it is usual for them to dismiss without serious attention the question as to whether such movements had any significance for contemporary Hebrew thought. Thus, W. F. Lofthouse wrote: 'From the sixth century onward, a new leaven was working in the world; and scholars would tell us that from Egypt, Persia, and Greece, to say nothing of influences coming from farther afield, the Jews received more than they ever gave . . . no serious attempt has ever been made to show anything comparable, outside Israel, with the profound religious insight that animated the three great prophets of the exile. . . .'[3] Yet in the sixth century B.C. non-Israelite teachers were also in search of solutions to the most vital problems of life. Zarathustra was rejecting the polytheistic worship of his people and was arriving at a conception of his god Ahura-Mazda as a being of Right and Truth. Buddha was enunciating the principles by which the evil and miseries of life could be abolished, while the Ionian philosophers were searching for the source and ground of being.

This was, moreover, a period of significant political changes in the Near East. New forces appeared on the horizon as the Scythians and Medes descended from their mountain homes to the plains of Mesopotamia. The great Assyrian empire which for centuries had been the dominant power was now disintegrating under their constant raids. The Chaldeans, who had long resented

---

[1] *The Truth of the Bible*, 1938, p. 132.   [2] Camb., 1950, p. 72.
[3] *After the Exile*, 1928, p. 61.

Assyrian domination, combined with the Medes and Scythians to bring about the fall of Nineveh in 612 B.C. Egypt had at this time recovered from a period of weakness and had established commercial relations with the enterprising Greeks. Indeed Necho wished to revive his nation's former greatness and in 609 led an army through Palestine hoping to establish a footing in Western Asia. At the battle of Carchemish (605), however, the combined efforts of the Medes and Chaldeans finally routed the Assyrians, and Necho was compelled to retire leaving Nebuchadrezzar the undisputed master of the field. Nebuchadrezzar quickly extended his rule over the west and within two decades had deported many of the Judeans to Babylon. But the Chaldean power which had become supreme at Carchemish lasted little more than half a century; for the Medes and Persians now appeared in history as a powerful and organised force under the leadership of Cyrus. In 539 Babylon fell to his armies, and the rulership of the ancient Near East finally passed out of the hands of the Semites. Thus in power as well as in thought the Indo-Europeans became prominent in history.

Changes of a political and intellectual nature were hence passing over the ancient world. From the Nile to the Tigris armies were on the march, and from the Pacific Ocean to the shores of Asia Minor the mind of man was astir.[1] An old age was passing away; new forces and new ideas were coming into being and were imparting freshness and vitality to an outworn and stagnant world. It was the beginning of the age of philosophy, science, and theology,[2] and marked the first step in man's advance from tradition and credulity to argument and reason. For the mind, emancipated from the fetters of mythology and superstition, was making inquiries into the nature of the universe and into the mystery and purpose of man's existence.[3] Referring to the 'time

[1] Cf. H. G. Wells, *A Short History of the World*, p. 95 (revised edn., Penguin Books, 1949).

[2] Herodotus, writing about 450 B.C., spoke of the formulation of the science of theology as 'unknown till yesterday' (Bk. 2, 53).

[3] 'This change of view is breath-taking. It transfers the problems of man in nature from the realm of faith and poetic intuition to the intellectual sphere.' (H. and H. A. Frankfort, *The Intellectual Adventure of Ancient Man*, Chicago, 1946, p. 376.)

when ... the foremost intellects of the race awaken out of the dream of mythology' R. M. Cornford said: 'They perceive that the imagery of myth has become incredible and fantastic; and they demand literal, matter-of-fact truth. This happened in sixth-century Ionia, and what the Western world calls philosophy or science was born. The philosophers, trying to think clearly, discard the old representations. The aura of associations is dispelled, and the abstract concept—the tool of the new kind of thought—begins to emerge.'[1] Man had now been transported into a new sphere where the struggle was no longer one of man with nature, but of man's attempt to reach and understand the unseen powers behind the phenomena of nature. Through the dictates of the moral and religious conscience, as well as by the efforts of the intellect, concepts of deity and of an ultimate reality were attained which disclosed the imperfections of tradition. And though some of these concepts may, according to our present standards, have been far short of that which approaches a true estimate of deity, they must be accepted as attempts to pass beyond the stage when the imposing objects of nature were invested with divine qualities. They represent the efforts of the early teachers of the race to launch out into the depths of thought and to reach an idea of the Infinite which transcends all forms of mundane existence.

This prominence of the exilic age over the centuries immediately before and after illustrates the falsity of the notion that advancement is a regular and constant factor in history. The steady and universal 'progress' and 'development' of the race as assumed by eighteenth- and nineteenth-century thinkers is scarcely vindicated by the moral and social events of history. That, however, there has been some advancement in thought and culture is amply testified by the course of the history of the world.[2] And this is no less true of the history of religions. There

---

[1] *The Unwritten Philosophy and Other Essays* (ed. W. K. C. Guthrie), Camb., 1950, p. 42.

[2] Commenting on the tendency towards the formation of culture Christopher Dawson remarked: 'It is impossible to deny the reality and importance of cultural progress. This progress is not, however, as philosophers of the eighteenth century believed, a continuous

is, however, a reluctance to think of any advancement that may
be discerned in the history of Hebrew religion in terms of progress or development due to the association of these terms with
the concepts of earlier rationalism. And because the term 'evolution' was originally applied by Darwin to the science of biology
there is a similar unwillingness to use such nomenclature in the
sphere of biblical thought. Discussing 'the particular and peculiar
evolution of biblical faith' G. E. Wright preferred the word
'epigenesis' to 'mutation', declaring that 'what is meant is a
radical revolution, as opposed to evolution'.[1] On the other hand
S. A. Cook could say: 'The modern way of viewing biblical
religion along evolutionary lines has become so firmly established that no one who has once discovered how it has enabled
him to understand the religious history of Israel will want or,
indeed, be able, to return to any earlier outlook.'[2] Similarly,
W. F. Albright, although a scholar of the conservative critical
type, could confess 'I am an evolutionist, but only in an organismic, not in a mechanical or melioristic sense. . . . The most
reasonable philosophy of history in my judgment is evolutionary
and . . . organismic.'[3] No careful observer of the historical scene
can fail to notice that there have been movements of thought,
however we wish to conceive of them, which have led to man's
higher conception of God. And no one would wish to deny that
the centuries which separate Moses from Deutero-Isaiah record
an advance in Israel's conception of her God. In the documents
pertaining to the early history of Israel we observe Yahweh in
operation within the boundaries of Canaan (e.g., Jud. 11 : 23–24);
in the literature of the reforming prophets we find Him exercising

and uniform movement common to the whole race. . . . It is rather an exceptional
condition, due to a number of distinct causes, which often operate irregularly and spas-
modically.' (*The Age of the Gods*, p. xvi, Lond., 1933.) So Gordon Childe said: 'Progress
is real if discontinuous. . . .' (*What Happened in History*, Penguin Books, 1952, p. 282.)

[1] *The Old Testament against its Environment*, Lond., 1950, p. 15, and note 11.

[2] *The Truth of the Bible*, p. 59.

[3] J.B.L., 59, 1940, p. 97. In his work entitled *The Evolution of Religion* Edward Caird
said with some justification: 'When Christ spoke of his own ethical doctrine as a fulfilment
of that which potentially or in germ was contained in the law . . . he gave a clearer
expression to the idea of development than it had ever before received, and even perhaps
than it has received till quite recent times.' (Vol. 1, p. 22, Glasgow, 1893.)

dominion from Greece to the Mediterranean and from Egypt to Assyria (Amos 9: 7; Is. 10: 5); but in the writings of Deutero-Isaiah we find a conception of Him as the Judge and Saviour of all the nations of the earth (Is. 45: 22). Yet this enrichment of Israel's knowledge of Yahweh did not take the form of a uniform advancement. Rather we observe periods of decline followed by periods of revival in which new and higher spiritual concepts emerge. This pattern of events cannot then be explained in terms of mechanical progress, but is due to the inspiration and success of certain religious leaders who appeared on the scene.

In Israel too we find that there were religious truths for which the historical environment was not ready. While the reforming prophets denounced the popular idolatrous worship and emphasised the moral demands of the holy God of Israel there were truths regarding His nature which were only first expounded during the exile. For the conditions and developments of the exile demanded a reorientation of the Hebrew mind on the being and nature of Yahweh. A conception of Him as the national God of Israel and as worshipped in accordance with the ritual of Canaan could prove but inadequate to the religious needs of the exilic community. Accordingly the genuine prophets of the day were confronted with the challenge of presenting to the exiles concepts of God requisite to their new circumstances. On removal from Judah the exiles were forthwith confronted with the problem of worship. They had hitherto worshipped Yahweh at the sanctuary in Jerusalem but now wondered if communion with the national God of Israel were at all possible on foreign soil (cf. e.g., Ps. 137: 4). By declaring, however, that Yahweh could be found wherever the heart of man sought Him sincerely Jeremiah (29: 13–14) exposed the limitations of the notion that He could be worshipped only in Palestine and that approach to Him lay through cultic channels. Again, adhering to the traditional belief that the sons suffer for the sins of the fathers (Ex. 20: 5; Num. 14: 18), the exiles interpreted their captivity as a punishment for the iniquities of the nation (Jer. 31: 29; Ezek. 18: 2). Believing that it was the nature of Yahweh to exact retribution

for such sins many of them now questioned His justice. Compelled, therefore, to address himself to this problem Ezekiel
preached the doctrine that God exacts retribution for individual
sins only, and that consequently the individual himself is responsible for any punishment he bears.

In exile the Israelites came into contact with an advanced culture
and with certain modes of thought which were at this time
current in Babylon. The splendour of their environment made
them wonder as to what power the national God of Israel could
exercise there, while the claims of contemporary thought
prompted reflection on the question of His ultimate sovereignty.
Indeed if the exiles were to continue their adherence to Yahweh
they needed some positive reassurance as to His power and
nature. Thus it was that using the methods and arguments of an
apologist Deutero-Isaiah demonstrated the inanity of the alleged
gods of Babylon and convincingly established the proposition
that Yahweh alone is God and that He is the Creator and Sustainer of man and the universe. Any fruitful discussion of his
teaching cannot therefore be indifferent to the ferment of
speculative and religious thought which was so much a feature of
his age.

II

AN AGE OF CHALLENGE AND CHANGE

IT is remarkable that while significant religious and intellectual movements were taking place in certain parts of the East during the sixth century B.C. the ancient civilisations of Mesopotamia and Egypt virtually came to an end at this same period. It is therefore proposed to consider here the causes which led to their decline and to indicate how their failure to meet the challenge of new forces led in turn to far-reaching political and cultural changes. It will be seen that while the final collapse came with the appearance of the overwhelming armies of the Persians there had been for some time an undermining of those elements which are essential to the continuance of a civilisation. For the structure of the civilisations of Mesopotamia and Egypt was based on principles which contained within them the seeds of their own destruction. Acquiring imperial greatness through conquest and plunder the Assyrians and Egyptians lacked the ability to consolidate their gains and stabilise their forces when other peoples became contenders in the political field. The individual, for centuries the slave of king and empire, subdued by the priesthood and oppressed by superstition, had little to support him when the old order was challenged from without. The signs of decay, long evident, had rapidly increased until in the sixth century a tired and outworn Babylon and Egypt contrasted strangely with the youthful vigour and creative thought of the Greeks and Persians. Thus the fall of Nineveh and the Assyrian and Egyptian defeat at Carchemish were among the most significant political events of the ancient world. They marked the end of a long epoch of Semitic and Egyptian supremacy and were the final indications that the vigorous Indo-Europeans were about to occupy the thrones from which Oriental monarchs had so long exercised their rule.

Decadent Mesopotamia

Mesopotamian civilisation was a highly organised and complex structure. It was based on the assumption that the influence of the gods pervaded every aspect of life and that the king was the divine viceregent on earth.[1] Obedience to the king and his officials, to the gods and their priests, became in consequence an established feature of the social fabric.[2] It was therefore essentially a society in which the community rather than the individual was recognised. Yet the individual did not complain. It was his accepted way of life and he had no option but to obey, for 'A young man must wholeheartedly obey the command of his god' and must 'truly proclaim the greatness of his god'.[3] This he could willingly do as long as life seemed secure and worthwhile. Sargon, Sennacherib, and Esarhaddon, as their inscriptions show, could all attribute their victories to their gods and think that they were the chosen men of their race.[4] And while the Assyrian empire was expanding and maintaining a position of supremacy the individual, too, gladly worshipped his god and willingly paid his dues. The conception of the state as belonging to and ruled by the gods was thus helpful in unifying the forces of the vast Assyrian empire. The kings, regarded as the human agents of the gods, pursued unhindered their ruthless policy of plunder and conquest. And although the problem of the righteous sufferer had long been experienced[5] yet, while the prosperity of the empire was assured the issues of life and the nature of the gods were not to be questioned.

[1] Cf. Henri Frankfort, *Kingship and the Gods*, 1941, p. 252.
[2] Cf. T. Jacobsen, *The Intellectual Adventure of Ancient Man*, 1946, p. 202.
[3] T. Jacobsen, op. cit., p. 204.
[4] See, e.g., 'Sargon's Inscriptions' (A.N.E.T., p. 286).
[5] E.g., in the hymn 'I will Praise the Lord of Wisdom', written towards the end of the second millennium B.C., the problem of the righteous sufferer and of the moral government of the world is raised. For text see A.N.E.T., pp. 434 f.

But when Sennacherib mounted the Assyrian throne in 705 he had some difficulty in maintaining the extensive imperial conquests of his predecessor Sargon. Israel as a state had succumbed to Sargon but now Judah, Babylon, and the states of Tyre and Sidon exhibited a restlessness which proved embarrassing to Sennacherib. It had been the policy of Assyria to deport the native inhabitants of subdued states and to replace them by captives from other places. A generation or so of such racial intermingling could only produce a population which had no particular loyalty to any country much less to the enslaving power of Assyria. It was therefore natural that these subject peoples should challenge Assyrian domination whenever opportunity arose. Moreover, towards the end of the seventh century some Indo-European tribes known as Cimmerians and Scythians[1] were descending from their northern homes to the more fertile plains and were raiding the Assyrian frontiers. The Medes and Elamites were now also successfully resisting the Assyrians and by 625 Cyaxeres had completely overthrown their authority in the East.[2] Thus raided by the Cimmerians and Scythians and attacked by the Medes and Chaldeans Assyria was forced to withdraw within her own cities and was compelled to defend her national boundaries.

With such visible signs of imperial disintegration it was inevitable that the gods who ordained and maintained the empire should themselves be regarded with some scepticism. The secession of many states and the consequent loss of revenue limited the economic resources of the nation. Taxation became higher for the ordinary citizen, while in such times of national crisis the temple taxes and the priestly dues could not be neglected. Yet the gods who had failed to protect the empire seemed now equally powerless to preserve the nation. The enemy had penetrated within its territories and the security of the individual was threatened. Less than a century earlier the boastful Rabshakeh could ask 'Has any of the gods of the nations ever delivered his

[1] Cf. Herodotus, Bk. 4, 1–143, where he is mainly concerned with the origin and habits of these peoples.

[2] Cf. Clemens Huart, *Ancient Persian and Iranian Civilisation* (Eng. trans.), 1927, pp. 28–30.

land out of the hand of the king of Assyria?' (2 Kgs. 18: 33).
But now god and king alike failed the expectations of the serious
individual who, thus frustrated, could only entertain a sceptical
attitude towards religious and moral values.

Already in the first millennium B.C. an attitude of cynicism
and doubt had pervaded Mesopotamian civilisation. Typical of
its kind is a dialogue between a master and his slave known as
'The Dialogue of Pessimism'.[1] In tones reminiscent of the author
of the biblical Ecclesiastes the dialogue represents all life as vain
and purposeless. Life at the palace, the pleasures of food and wine,
and the excitement of the chase all fail to give satisfaction.[2]
Significant, however, is the despairing attitude towards religion
as the lines quoted here illustrate:

> I will offer a sacrifice to my god. . . .
> No, servant, a sacrifice to my god will I not offer.
> Do not offer (it), my Lord, do not offer (it).
> You may teach a god to trot after you like a dog
> When he requires of you, (saying)
> '(Celebrate) my ritual' or 'do not inquire
> (By requesting an oracle)' or anything else.[3]

Indifference to the claims of his god is now followed by his doubt
as to the point of doing alms in the form of giving food to his
country:

> I shall give food to our country:
> Give it, my Lord, give it . . .
> No, servant, food to my country I shall not give.[4]

The master then considers if he should do something helpful for
his country, but finally decides against it:

> Servant . . . I will do something helpful for my country.
> Do (it) my Lord, do (it).
> The man who does something helpful for his country—
> His helpful deed is placed in the bowl of Marduk.

---

[1] Cf. T. Jacobsen, op. cit., p. 216.
[2] Dialogue, lines 1–20, as trans. by R. H. Pfeiffer, in A.N.E.T., pp. 437–438.
[3] Dialogue, lines 60–69, p. 438.   [4] Dialogue, lines 70–75, p. 438.

No, servant, I will not do something helpful for my country.
Do it not, my Lord, do it not.
Climb the mounds of ancient ruins and walk about:
Look at the skulls of late and early (men);
Who (among them) is an evildoer, who a public benefactor?[1]

As he surveys the ruins of ancient cities, representative of the disintegrating forces in life and symbolic of his own civilisation, he regards as transitory and insignificant the good that a man may do in his lifetime. Indeed, in such an empty and dissatisfying world the only wise course to take is to escape from it. And so to the question 'What is good?' the only logical answer is:

To break my neck, your neck,
Throw (both) into the river—(that) is good.[2]

But even now the master is not sure what awaits him at death, and so again shows his indecision by remarking:

No, servant, I shall kill you and send you ahead of me.

But, in accordance with the characteristic mood of the day, the author of the Dialogue could only allow the slave to reply:

'(Then) would my Lord (wish to) live even three days after me?'[3]

Life had thus become so intolerable that whatever awaited the individual at death it was unthinkable to endure even another three days of misery on earth.

This attitude to life continued until in the seventh century B.C.[4] we find, in 'A Dialogue about Human Misery', a more critical attitude towards the gods and an increasing awareness of the problem of evil:

The god brought me scarcity instead of wealth [line 75][5] . . .
Let me forget the votive gifts of the god,
Trample upon ritual prescriptions [lines 134–5] . . .
The godless, the scoundrel, who has acquired wealth,
The murderer (with) his weapon pursues him [lines 237–8] . . .
The god does not stop the advance of the Serrabu-demon [line 244].

---

[1] Dialogue, lines 76–84, p. 438.   [2] Dialogue, lines 85–86.   [3] Dialogue, lines 87–88.
[4] For the date, see R. H. Pfeiffer, A.N.E.T., p. 438, note 1.
[5] R. H. Pfeiffer, ibid., p. 439.

But this negative attitude to life pervaded all classes of society. According to Strabo the inscription upon the tomb of king Ashurbanipal (Sardanapulus) was: 'Eat drink and be merry for all things are not worth' a snap of the fingers.[1] Despite his great interest in literature and his success as a ruler he found little of intrinsic value in life beyond the pleasures of eating and drinking. After Ashurbanipal's death in about 630 the empire disintegrated rapidly, and his successors had even less reason to be satisfied with life.

As the 'Dialogue about Human Misery' shows, the ordinary individual now regarded religion with extreme scepticism. The sacrifices and libations offered to the gods proved so ineffective that they might as well be trampled under foot. Life, too, was so manifestly composed of more evil than good that the influence of the gods was regarded as negligible. Thus it was that the individual, disillusioned by king and god, and deprived of all personal resourcefulness by the highly organised nature of his society and environment, was now at this critical juncture of his nation's history frustrated by the exigencies of time and fate. It was consequently a demoralised and indifferent individual, and an exhausted and decadent nation, which met the combined forces of the Scythians, Medes, and Chaldeans at the outskirts of Nineveh in 612 B.C. The fall of the city and the destruction of the Assyrians is described by a contemporary chronicle: 'The city was seized and a great defeat he inflicted (upon the) entire population. On that day Sinsharishkun,[2] king of Assyria fled. . . . Many prisoners of the city, beyond counting, they carried away. The city (they turned) into ruin—hills and heaps (of debris)'.[3] A contemporary Hebrew prophet similarly remarked: 'This is the exultant city that dwelt secure. . . . What a desolation she has become, a lair for wild beasts ' (Zeph. 2: 15). Another

---

[1] *Geography of Strabo*, Bk. VI, 14, 5, 9 (Loeb Class. Lib., 1929, p. 341).

[2] He died during the fall of Nineveh (C. J. Gadd, *The Fall of Nineveh*, Lond., 1923, pp. 4, 13). His successor, Ashuruballit II, the last king of Assyria, managed, however, to maintain himself for a few more years in Harran. ('New Bab. Chron.', line 50; Gadd, op. cit., pp. 23–24, 40.)

[3] 'New Babylonian Chronicle', as trans. by A. L. Oppenheim, A.N.E.T., pp. 304–305; see also C. J. Gadd, *The Fall of Nineveh*, p. 40.

Hebrew prophet addressed the smitten nation thus: 'Wasted is
Nineveh; who will bemoan her? Whence shall I seek comforters
for her? ... Your shepherds are asleep, O King of Assyria, your
nobles slumber. Your people are scattered on the mountains, with
none to gather them ...' (Nah. 3: 7, 18, R.S.V.).

The Chaldeans became the immediate heirs of the Assyrians,
and establishing their capital in Babylon founded the Neo-
Babylonian empire. Under the vigorous leadership of Nebuchadrezzar Mesopotamian civilisation was prolonged, but on his
death in 562 it was evident that the empire could survive only a
few decades. For it was of necessity composed of the dying
elements of Mesopotamian culture, and the Babylonians now
manifested this decadence in their distrust of the reigning kings.
Awel-Marduk succeeded his father Nebuchadrezzar, but according to the Babylonian historian, Berossus, 'he governed public
affairs after an illegal and impure manner'.[1] Within a year of his
accession he was murdered by his brother-in-law, Neriglissar,
who himself usurped the throne. Although claiming that the god
Marduk decreed his accession[2] he lived to reign for only four
years (560–557) leaving the throne to his young son, Lebashi-
Marduk. The usurping dynasty was no more successful than the
preceding one, for after a chaotic reign of a few months, the
ruling classes deposed the young king and tormented him to
death 'owing to his depraved disposition and evil practices'.[3]
According to Berossus the conspirators now 'got together and by
common consent, put the crown upon the head of Nabonnedus,
a man of Babylon, and who belonged to that insurrection'.[4]

Nabonidus was the last king of Babylon. It was therefore during
his reign that the city fell on its most evil days and passed out of
Semitic rulership. There has, consequently, been much specula-

[1] Apud Josephus, *Contra Apionem*, Bk. I, 20, trans. by Whiston (Berossus, a Chaldean
of the third cen. B.C., wrote a history of Babylon, *Chaldaica*, comprising some three books,
cf. Jos., ibid.).   [2] Cf. A.N.E.T., p. 309 (iii, lines 5–6).

[3] Berossus, ibid. The Nabonidus Inscription also referred to him as 'a minor (who) had
not (yet) learned how to behave' (A.N.E.T., p. 309, iv). See *Babylonian Chronology
626 B.C.–A.D. 45*, by R. A. Parker and Waldo Dubberstein, Chicago, 1942, p. 10, for the
view that his reign was only of two months' duration.

[4] Berossus, ibid. (trans. by Whiston).

tion on the character of this king, and on the circumstances which led to his accession. It has been suggested that Nabonidus was appointed by members of the Babylonian priesthood.[1] And the intrigues of the priesthood which persisted throughout the preceding reigns together with the consideration that Nabonidus himself is thought to have been of priestly origin[2] naturally lend support to this view. But there are also grounds for thinking that the people of Babylon had some voice in the choice of Nabonidus. Contemporary documentary evidence represents Nabonidus saying at his accession: 'They carried me into the palace and all prostrated themselves to my feet . . . greeting me again and again as king. (Thus) I was elevated to rule the country by the order of my lord Marduk, and (therefore) I shall obtain whatever I desire —there shall be no rival of mine.'[3] This is in no way contrary to the evidence furnished by Berossus. Both sources indicate that the Babylonians had become dissatisfied with the rulership of Labashi-Marduk, and that Nabonidus commanded the support of a wide section of the population. It was evident to even the most indifferent citizen that the chaos and incompetence which characterised the reigns of kings since Nebuchadrezzar could not be allowed to continue and that a man of some promise and ability was now needed to govern the country. Nabonidus seemed to possess all the desired qualities. He was of noble and honourable birth,[4] and had passed some years of his life in courtly circles. He had also some claim to a knowledge of government affairs, for Herodotus records that he was the Babylonian representative at the conclusion of a peace treaty between the Medes and the Lydians in 585.[5] Consequently with some thirty years' connection with affairs of state he no doubt as 'a man of Babylon' could only

---

[1] E.g., S. H. Hooke, *Babylonian and Assyrian Religion*, p. 54; R. P. Dougherty, *Archives from Erech*, Oxford, 1923, p. 19.

[2] Cf. The Eski-Harran Inscription (A.N.E.T., p. 311 (b), para. 1 f.); also P. Dhorme, R.B., 1908, pp. 130–135; L. W. King, *A History of Babylon*, 2, p. 281; R. P. Dougherty, op. cit., pp. 18 f. See, however, Julius Lewy, 'The Late Assyro-Babylonian Cult of the Moon and its Culmination at the Time of Nabonidus', H.U.C.A., 19, 1945–46 (pp. 405–489), p. 407.   [3] A.N.E.T., p. 309, v.

[4] See R. P. Dougherty, *Nabonidus and Belshazzar*, New Haven, 1929, pp. 16 f.; also J. Lewy, loc. cit., pp. 410–411, 418 n. 74.

[5] Her. 1, 74: Cf. also R. P. Dougherty, *Nabonidus and Belshazzar*, p. 36.

view with disapproval the anarchy which prevailed during the reigns of Awel-Marduk, Neriglissar, and Labashi-Marduk; and we can thus understand Berossus' reference to him as being among those who disapproved of the government of Labashi-Marduk. The Babylonians now naturally reflected on the prosperous reign of Nebuchadrezzar[1] which contrasted so strongly with the ineptitude of his successors. When therefore a man was available with such accomplishments as Nabonidus, and who moreover had probably close family connections with Nebuchadrezzar,[2] it was only natural that his candidature for the office of king should be adopted 'by common consent'. Thus it would seem that Nabonidus was not so much the choice of the priesthood, but was elected by the people on the ground that he was the last surviving link with Nebuchadrezzar, and was raised to the throne of Babylon in the hope that his rule would recapture some of the confidence and stability which characterised the foundation of the Neo-Babylonian empire.[3]

But whatever the precise circumstances of his election it is clear that on his accession he was faced with both religious and economic problems. Recognising that the Babylonian religion with its many and diverse elements of polytheism stood in some danger from the positive and constructive thought which was spreading in the world of his day, Nabonidus raised the ancient Assyrian god Sin to the supreme place in the Babylonian pantheon. Accordingly he restored the temple of Ehulhul in Harran[4] and renovated temples to Assyrian deities in the regions of Babylon.[5] This, however, could hardly be expected to meet with the approval of

[1] Cf. his Inscriptions in A.N.E.T., pp. 307–308; also Her. 1, 178–183, for the sumptuous manner in which he adorned Babylon; see also G. Contenau, op. cit., pp. 37–38.

[2] See R. P. Dougherty, *Nabonidus and Belshazzar*, pp. 60 f., for the view that he was son-in-law of Nebuchadrezzar, and that the 'sagacious queen Nitocris' (Her. 1, 185) was his wife; and Sidney Smith, *Babylonian Historical Texts*, Lond., 1924, for the theory that Nabonidus was the son of Nitocris who was Nebuchadrezzar's favourite wife, pp. 37, 43.

[3] Cf. S. Smith, op. cit., pp. 32 and 42, for reasons why Nabonidus could scarcely be the choice of the priesthood.

[4] 'Building Inscriptions of Nabonidus', A.N.E.T., 311 (x).

[5] A.N.E.T., p. 311 (ix); also p. 311b for Eski-Harran Inscription; C. J. Gadd, *Royal Inscriptions from Ur* (with Legrain), 1928, no. 187; A. H. Sayce, *Records of the Past*, vol. V, pp. 171–174 (lines 1–65).

his Babylonian subjects.[1] We are therefore not surprised to read of the discontent of the people on religious grounds and of charges of impiety being made against him.[2] Moreover, he enthusiastically observed the worship of Sin in Arabia,[3] while neglecting the observance of the New Year Festival in Babylon.[4] In the fourth year of his reign (552) we read that Nabonidus 'set out on a distant journey. The forces of Akkad advanced with him, towards Tema in Ammurru he set his face.'[5] This place is identified with Taima, an oasis in the desert of Southern Arabia.[6] The exact object of his visit is unknown; it has been suggested that it was an attempt to control the trade routes of the Near Eastern world,[7] but Julius Lewy has recently argued that it 'was dictated by religious considerations'.[8] After about eight years, however,[9] the local tribes under the incentives of the Persians became hostile to the Babylonian forces,[10] and Nabonidus was forced to withdraw to Babylon which was itself shortly to fall before the Persian armies.

We cannot here pursue the character and reign of Nabonidus further, but it is evident that, contrary to general expectations, he was not able to restore the political power of Babylon or the vitality of an exhausted nation. He was preceded by weak rulers who were further impeded by the intrigues and fears of a declining people. Elected to power in 556 by a surge of national feeling, Nabonidus must have been aware that his accession was but the frenzied expression of a people bordering on the verge of moral

---

[1] Cf. J. Lewy, loc. cit., pp. 487–489.

[2] 'Persian Verse Account', col. v, lines 14–18 (S. Smith, *Bab. Hist. Texts*, p. 90).

[3] S. Smith, *Isaiah, Chapters XL–LV* (Schweich Lects., 1940), pp. 40, 42; J. Lewy, loc. cit., p. 441.

[4] 'Nabonidus Chronicle', col 2, lines 5–24; cf. also 'A Persian Verse Account of Nabonidus', col. 2, lines 10–11 (S. Smith, *Bab. Hist. Texts*, p. 88).

[5] 'Persian Verse Account', lines 21–23 (S. Smith, *Bab. Hist. Texts*, p. 88).

[6] J. Lewy, loc. cit., pp. 441–450.

[7] S. Smith, *Isaiah, Chapters XL–LV*, pp. 37–40; cf. R. P. Dougherty, *Nabonidus and Belshazzar*, pp. 138–160, for the possibility that Nabonidus went to Arabia to establish his sovereignty over the West.

[8] Loc. cit., p. 438.

[9] 'Nabonidus Chronicle', 3, lines 5–6 (S. Smith, *Bab. Hist. Texts*, pp. 102, 109, 117).

[10] S. Smith, op. cit., pp. 44–45; R. P. Dougherty, op. cit., pp. 161–162.

2

and economic collapse.[1] Yet, as though by the irony of a strange
fate, the Babylonians were but further frustrated by the rulership
of Nabonidus. For in absenting himself for so long from his
capital, returning home only when expelled from Arabia, and by
ignoring the claims of the Babylonian gods, his subjects finally
lost all moral and religious fortitude.

Meanwhile new forces were being organised in the East and
ominous shadows were cast on the rapidly declining Semitic
power. Cyrus had united the Persian tribes[2] and in 550 successfully repudiated the sovereignty of his Median overlord,
Astyages.[3] He now incorporated the Medes under his leadership
and united the Aryan peoples of Iran into a formidable force
expressing the sovereignty and power of Persia. With a rapidity
unparalleled in ancient military history the conquests of Cyrus
increased until in 547 he brought the whole of the Lydian empire
under his control.[4]

Such was the strength of the foe which was soon to challenge
the decadent power of Babylon. Since the days of the Scythian
raids there were many foreigners within the Babylonian empire,
and these, added to the numbers brought there during years of
deportation, constituted a section of the population which could
only regard with indifference the prospect of an invading army.
The Babylonians themselves, being but the survivors of a long
declining Mesopotamian civilisation, had now reached a stage of
inertia which rendered them incapable of offering any effective
resistance. Hence a contemporary record tells us that when the
disciplined Persian army crossed the Tigris, 'Sippar was seized
without battle. Nabonidus fled ... And the army of Cyrus
entered Babylon without battle.'[5] So in 539 Babylon, rent by
internal dissensions and divided interests, fell ingloriously and

---

[1] Cf. R. P. Dougherty, *Records from Erech*, 1920, no. 154, for economic conditions
in Babylonia at this time; cf. also the Verse Account, lines 1–16 (S. Smith, *Bab. Hist.
Texts*, p. 87).

[2] Her. I, 126–129.

[3] A. T. Olmstead, *The History of the Persian Empire*, p. 37.

[4] A. T. Olmstead, op. cit., pp. 38–40. See also Her. I, 79–91.

[5] 'Nabonidus Chronicle', col. 3, lines 14–18; cf. also Xenophon, 'Cyropaedia',
VII, v, 17–34; Jer. 51: 30–32.

passed with all the grandeur of her ancient civilisation into the hands of the Persians.

Decadent Egypt

Forces similar to those which proved destructive of Mesopotamian civilisation also combined to bring about the decline of Egypt. A nation with a long and brilliant history, her place in the world was not seriously challenged until the restless Amarna Age. Her possessions in Asia were then coveted by the Hittites, and thereafter Egypt itself was exposed to the threats of the Sea Peoples, Libyans, and Assyrians.[1] In order to meet these dangers from without the country was organised with a view to maintaining its unity. It was a natural instinct which prompted this unification, and it might have proved advantageous to the Egyptians had not the basis of its unity been the god-king.[2] The dangers which threatened the land were now interpreted as an indication of neglect of the national gods. Consequently the priests, who were the natural representatives of the Pharaoh, advocated a more elaborate recognition of the claims of the gods. Many new temples were founded and were generously endowed with lands and furnishings.[3] Thus it was that 'the previously modest temples in Egypt grew in physical size, in personnel, in land, and in total property, until they became the dominating factor in Egyptian political, social, and economic life'.[4] At length the power of the priesthood became so great that in 1085, Hrihor, a high-priest of Amun of Thebes, forced the Rameside dynasty to abdicate in his favour.[5] The line of priest-kings thus established

[1] Cf. J. A. Wilson, 'Egypt', in the *Intell. Adven. of Anc. Man*, p. 111; also J. H Breasted, *History of Egypt*, Lond., 1906, pp. 464 f.

[2] 'Pharaoh was not mortal, but a god. This was the fundamental concept of Egyptian kingship, that Pharaoh was of divine essence, a god incarnate. . . . It is wrong to speak of a deification of Pharaoh. His divinity was not proclaimed at a certain moment. . . . His coronation was not an apotheosis but an epiphany.' (Henri Frankfort, *Kingship and the Gods*, p. 5.) Cf. also C. J. Gadd, *Ideas of Divine Rule in the Ancient East*, Lond., 1948, p. 45.

[3] See J. H. Breasted, *Ancient Records of Egypt*, IV, pp. 87–198 (1906); also J. Černý, *Ancient Egyptian Religion*, 1952, pp. 115–116.

[4] J. A. Wilson, op. cit., p. 112.

[5] *When Egypt Ruled the East*, by G. Steindorff and K. C. Steele, 1952, p. 270.

further emphasised the place of the temple in the national life. The history of the Egyptian nation from this time till its dissolution is therefore essentially a story of the submission of the people to the demands of the temple and its representatives. The principle of group solidarity in the interests of national security became a cardinal doctrine of the priests with a consequent suppression of all forms of individual expression.[1]

Homage to the deity was regarded as the first duty of man. Accordingly in 'The Instruction of Ani', which may be assigned to the period of the eleventh to the eighth centuries B.C.,[2] we read:

> Celebrate the feast of thy God and repeat it at its season.
> God is angry at them who disregard him.[3]

Passive, silent resignation to fate was expected from all members of society. The same text enjoins:

> Do not talk a lot. Be silent, and thou wilt be happy.
> Do not be garrulous. The dwelling of god,
> Its abomination is clamour.[4]

Rather, man's concern should be to offer sacrifice with due reverence and decorum:

> Make offering to thy god, and beware of sins against him.
> Thou shouldst not inquire about his affairs. . . .
> Do not approach him (too closely) to carry him.
> Thou shouldst not disturb the veil;
> Beware of exposing what it shelters.
> Let thy eye have regard to the nature of his anger,
> And prostrate thyself in his name.[5]

In 'The Instruction of Amenemopet', belonging probably to the seventh and sixth centuries,[6] we find the ideal of the true

---

[1] Cf. J. A. Wilson, op. cit., p. 112.
[2] J. A. Wilson, A.N.E.T., p. 420.
[3] J. A. Wilson, ibid. (iii).
[4] A.N.E.T., ibid. (iv). Cf. also 'Chester Beatty Papyrus' (Third Series), no. IV, 5, where the god is represented as 'loving the silent man more than him who is loud of voice' (trans. by A. H. Gardiner, *Hieratic Papyri in the British Museum*, vol. 1, 1935, p. 30).
[5] Ani, vii, 12 f., A.N.E.T. (Wilson), p. 420.
[6] J. A. Wilson, A.N.E.T., p. 421.

worshipper. In contrast to the man of temper and passion who comes into the temple:

> The truly silent man holds himself apart.
> He is like a tree growing in a garden. . . .
> Its fruit is sweet; its shade is pleasant.[1]

Moreover, man was thought to be in a state of personal helplessness and capable of achieving nothing by himself, for:

> The god is ever in his success,
> Man is ever in his failure.[2]

Man may voice his opinion on certain issues, but to no effect, because,

> The words which men say are one thing,
> The things which god doeth another.[3]

The acts of the god and the nature of his being are not open to question by man:

> Look not at a place thou shouldst not know,
> Question not god.[4]

In Amenemopet we further find the injunction:

> Do not discover for thy own self the will of god,
> Without (reference to) Fate and Fortune.[5]

On the contrary,

> There is no ignoring Fate and Fortune . . .
> (For) every man belongs to his (appointed) hour.[6]

In this deterministic conception of life, man, weak and helpless in himself, had perforce to seek the comfort and advice of the gods. The great and powerful national gods may be too occupied with the affairs of state, or too remote in their unapproachable

[1] Amen. iv, 7 f., A.N.E.T. (Wilson), p. 422.
[2] Amen. xviii, 14-15, as trans. by F. L. Griffith, J.E.A., 12, 1926, p. 216.
[3] F. L. Griffith, ibid. (18, 16-17).
[4] Beatty Papyrus, IV, 5, 1 f., as ed. by Gardiner, op. cit., p. 42.
[5] Amen. xx, 15-16, A.N.E.T. (Wilson), p. 424.
[6] Amen. vii, 11-13, A.N.E.T., p. 422.

splendour, but there were several minor gods with whom attachments might be made and mercy sought.[1]

It is obvious that a civilisation so constituted could survive only as long as the empire, conceived of as under the guidance and protection of the gods, continued to exist. Once, however, the nation's stability declined and was threatened with disaster from without, the people accepted it as the inexorable decree of Fate. The emphasis of the priests on deferred hopes and a promise of good things in another world further served to induce a spirit of passivity and resignation in the individual. Thus, the Libyans and Ethiopians in turn succeeded in exercising their influence over Egypt, until in 671 Esarhaddon reduced it to an Assyrian province.[2]

A temporary revival was effected under Psammetichus, the founder of the Saite dynasty, but it is significant that this ruler was not a pure Egyptian, being descended from the Libyan chiefs of Sais.[3] Moreover, he was dependent on Greek mercenary troops, and not on the native Egyptians, for his success in overcoming the Assyrians.[4] Indeed, in so far as Egyptian militarism expressed itself at all it was in the opposition of the representatives of the local dynasts to the regime inaugurated by Psammetichus. He was therefore burdened not only with the task of restoring peace and order in the nation, but was compelled to rely on the support of his foreign legionaries to maintain himself on the throne.[5] And although Psammetichus reorganised the Egyptian state and established prosperous trading relations with the progressive Greeks,[6] he could not succeed in achieving a genuine internal renaissance. For, whatever commercial prosperity he achieved, the people showed none of that vigour and vitality necessary to national recovery. On the contrary, conscious of their waning powers and

[1] J. A. Wilson, *Intell. Adven. of Anc. Man*, p. 117.

[2] S. Smith, *Bab. Hist. Texts*, pp. 3–4; F. K. Kienitz, *Die politische Geschichte Ägyptens vom 7. bis zum 4. Jahrhundert vor der Zeitwende*, Berlin, 1953, p. 8.

[3] Diodorus 1, 66, 8; see also Adolf Erman, *Life in Ancient Egypt*, Eng. tr. by H. M. Tirard, Lond., 1894, p. 50.

[4] Cf. Diod. 1, 66, 1.

[5] Her. 2, 152, 3; Diod. 1, 67, 2. Cf. also F. K. Kienitz, op. cit., p. 37.

[6] Diod. 1, 66, 9.

sceptical of the present and future, they now tried to fortify themselves by reflecting on the greatness that was once Egypt's. The
security of the period before the establishment of the Empire
became the particular focus of their attention, and they tried to
adopt the fashions and crafts of those days.[1] But, far from being
the spontaneous development of new forms, it was but the slavish
and archaic imitation of a vanished age.[2] Yet in architecture, art,
and orthography the Egyptians reverted to the styles of former
years.[3]

In matters of religion, too, the same conscious archaising is
discernible. The Egyptian pantheon was purged of all current
deities and the ritual of worship was conducted in the most ancient
manner. Wealthy merchants had the tombs of ancient kings
excavated, and engaged artists to reproduce both the texts and
script for use on their own tombs. 'The Book of the Dead', the
burial literature of ancient Egypt, was now finally revised and
considerable additions made to it. The worship of the old gods
was also revived and their tombs and temples were artistically
restored.[4]

In consequence of the emphasis laid on the revival of the old
religion and on the restoration of ancient temples, the priests
assumed a new importance and took every advantage of the
opportunities which their venerated position offered.[5] With
elaborate ceremony and pomp they conducted the state religion
now immeasurably enhanced by the introduction of ancient
rituals. Their claims to learning were also considerable, as their
office demanded efficiency in the script and language in which the
old liturgies were written.[6] Perusal of these archaic texts resulted

---

[1] 'It was as if a degenerate and worn-out England of the future, tired of imperial pomp,
were to go back for her inspiration to the Anglo-Saxon period, were to imitate that period
in every way, in art, in costume, and in manners, to replace the dignitaries of the present
day by "ealdormen", "jarls", and "thegns", and substitute for the Imperial Parliament
an English comic-opera "Witenagemot".' (H. R. Hall, *Ancient History of the Near East*.
Lond., 9th edn., 1936, p. 519.)

[2] J. H. Breasted, *History of Egypt*, Lond., 1900, p. 570.

[3] Cf. F. K. Kienitz, op. cit., pp. 50–51.

[4] See J. H. Breasted, *Ancient Records*, vol. IV, nos. 965–966, p. 493.

[5] Diod. 1, 73, 2.

[6] Cf. Diod., ibid.; J. H. Breasted, *History of Egypt*, p. 576.

in the fabrication of absurd mythologies designed to give inviolable antiquity to the office of priesthood as well as to claim ancient precedence for the ceremonies now practised. In the history of Herodotus we read: 'The priests wear linen only, and shoes of byblus, and are not permitted to wear any other garments or other shoes. They wash themselves in cold water twice every day, and twice every night; and, in a word, they use a number of ceremonies. On the other hand, they enjoy no slight advantages, for they do not consume or spend any of their private property; but sacred food is cooked for them, and a great quantity of beef and geese is allowed each of them every day, and wine from the grape is given them. . . . The service of each god is performed, not by one, but by many priests, of whom one is chief priest; and when one of them dies, his son is put in his place.'[1] The priests had not only established for themselves lucrative and hereditary positions, but according to Diodorus, 'They pay no taxes of any kind and in repute and power are second after the king.'[2] Having thus attained to such a place of prominence in the nation they were able to wield an unwholesome and oppressive power over the individual.

The Egypt of the seventh and sixth centuries B.C. had therefore little to offer the ordinary Egyptian citizen. He lived in an archaic and artificial civilisation, in a society dominated by the priesthood, and was largely dependent for his livelihood on the commerce of the Greeks and Phoenicians. And while Psammetichus I and his successor Necho made some attempts to regain lost possessions in Syria and Palestine,[3] the army, consisting mostly of hirelings, was but little interested in the recovery of an Egyptian empire. This dependence on Greek mercenaries and Greek merchandise continued for over a century until by the time of Amassis (568–526) the Greeks had established themselves permanently in the port of Naucratis on the Nile Delta.[4]

But while the vitality and character of the Egyptian national life was degenerating Cyrus was making rapid conquests in the north-east. In quick succession the empires of Lydia and Babylonia

---

[1] Her. 2, 37.   [2] Diod. 1, 73, 5.   [3] Her. 2, 159.   [4] Her. 2, 178.

fell before his armies, and his rule now extended to Phoenicia and Arabia. It was inevitable that this new and irresistible power of the East should turn towards Egypt, that land of surprise and wonders so inviting to conquest and plunder.[1] It was consequently with some anxiety that Amassis watched the movements of Cyrus and anticipated his designs on Egypt. In a desperate effort to save his country he extended his alliance with Greece and decided to finance his forces from the temple treasuries. But the priests, whose office and power were only recently enhanced, objected to this use of their funds and reacted by undermining the loyalty of the native troops.

Cyrus was not, however, destined to enter this land of promise. But his son Cambyses was no less determined in his desire for imperial conquest. He had already the Phoenician fleet at his command, and had made arrangements with the Arabs for the supply of water to his troops during their march across the desert to Egypt.[2] With such precautions the success of his campaign against the Egyptians was assured. The hand of death mercifully removed Amassis from the scene of impending disaster; and his son Psammetichus III inherited a kingdom which was powerless to meet the threat of invasion. When, therefore, Cambyses appeared in 525 at the head of a powerful army, Egypt, long exploited for the maintenance of priests and mercenaries, lay prostrate at his feet.

Thus after a long and varied record the great power of Egypt had drawn to a close, and the throne of the Pharaoh was occupied by a foreigner. Her part in the ancient world was played, and, like Nineveh and Babylon, she was numbered with the fallen. It was accordingly with true prophetic insight that Ezekiel had earlier said: 'There shall be no more a prince out of the land of Egypt' (30: 13).

Conclusions

Our consideration of the causes which led to the decadence of both the Mesopotamian and Egyptian civilisations leads to the

---

[1] Herodotus said of Egypt: 'It possesses more wonders than any other country and exhibits greater works than can be described' (2, 35).　　　[2] Her. 3, 4–7.

conclusion that the limitations imposed on the individual contributed more than any other cause to that decadence. The theocratic conception of the state whereby its organisation was regarded as the visible expression of the will of the gods allowed no place to the voice or expression of the individual. Gradually acquiring a position of prominence the priests, becoming hereditary as well as professional, claimed the exclusive right of access to the deity and of interpreting his dispositions towards his worshippers. In such a society it was impossible for the individual either to manifest independence of thought or to initiate a movement towards religious reform.

This situation contrasts sharply with the tendency towards individualism and freedom of religious thought which, apart from the challenging message of the exilic prophets, we find elsewhere in the East during these critical years. Thus in about the year 588 B.C.[1] Zarathustra, the prophet of Persia, entered on his mission in which he preached a revolutionary view of religion. Far from regarding the priests of his day as the guardians of sacred truth he subjected them to the most severe and destructive criticism.[2] Condemning the current notions of deity he conceived of his god Ahura-Mazda as primarily a god of goodness and truth.[3] Indeed so insistent was he on this property of Ahura that he was compelled to account for the 'bad' in life by attributing it to the Evil One, thus postulating a dualism of a good and an evil power as the source of all things.[4] But while there appeared to be as much evil as good in life, man was not thereby to regard evil as an insuperable power from which there was no escape. On the contrary, recognising the entity of the individual, Zarathustra taught that man had freedom to choose between good and evil. For Ahura granted man 'capacities to act and true doctrines to guide so that one could choose beliefs at will . . . according to his own heart and mind'.[5] Hence belief in the faculty of the freedom of

---

[1] See W. B. Henning, *Zoroaster*, Oxford, 1951, pp. 35–41; Jack Finegan, *The Archaeology of World Religions*, 1952, pp. 80–81.

[2] Yasna 46, 11; 48, 10; 51, 14: cf. also 32, 12, 15.

[3] Yasna 31, 7–8; 46, 9; 48, 3 passim.   [4] Yasna 30, 1–11.

[5] Yasna 31, 11–12, as trans. by D. F. A. Bode and P. Nanavutty in *Songs of Zarathustra*, Allen & Unwin, Lond., 1952, p. 54.

the will which Zarathustra regarded as 'a divine dispensation surpassing all others'[1] encouraged the individual to oppose evil and to hope for eventual victory over it. This was, however, an inspiration denied to the Babylonians and Egyptians with their more fatalistic view of life. Some twenty years later[2] Gautama Buddha preached an equally revolutionary doctrine in north-eastern India. For he not only questioned the dogma of the priests or Brahmans but was even sceptical of the existence of the great god Brahma himself.[3] Refusing to recognise the social distinctions of caste and other tenets of the priests[4] he enunciated to a disillusioned people his Noble Aryan Truth: 'This is that Aryan eightfold path, to wit, right view, right aspiration, right speech, right doing, right livelihood, right effort, right mindfulness, right rapture.'[5] By attempting to practise this ideal man would do much to abolish the evils and miseries of life.

Of the speculations in Greece at this time Cicero significantly remarked: 'Nearly every one of those Seven whom the Greeks called "wise" took an important part in the affairs of government.'[6] Thales, 'the wisest of the Seven',[7] was an engineer, and Anaximander a map-maker; but these secular occupations did not hinder them from entering the realms of the sacred and rejecting traditional cosmogonies in favour of those based on scientific observations. In Egypt a man was told, 'Question not god',[8] neither 'Inquire about the nature of his affairs',[9] and in Mesopotamia the fear of the gods forbade any scrutiny of their nature; but Xenophanes of sixth-century Greece could say:

> Homer and Hesiod have ascribed to the gods all things that are a disgrace among mortals, stealings, and adulteries, and deceptions of one another.[10]

---

[1] Yasna 51, 1 (*Songs of Zarathustra*, p. 99).

[2] About 567 B.C.; see Jack Finegan, op. cit., p. 248.

[3] *The Bible of the World*, ed. by R. O. Ballou, Lond., 1940, pp. 262–263.

[4] *The Bible of the World*, p. 303.   [5] *The Bible of the World*, p. 248.

[6] *De Republica*, I, 7.   [7] Cicero, *De Legibus*, 2, 11.

[8] 'Chester Beatty Papyrus', IV, 5, 1 f., as ed. by A. H. Gardiner, *Hieratic Papyri in the British Museum* (Third Series), vol. I, 1935, p. 42.

[9] A.N.E.T. (Wilson), p. 424.

[10] Fragment 11 as trans. by John Burnet, *Early Greek Philosophy*, 3rd edn., 1920, p. 119.

Contemptuous of popular belief he could say with some satirical force:

> Mortals deem that the gods are begotten as they are, and have clothes like theirs and voice and form.[1]

He scorned the notion, so characteristic of Mesopotamian and Egyptian belief, that the gods have always enlightened men, and welcomed the spirit of independent personal inquiry:

> The gods have not revealed all things to men from the beginning, but by seeking men find out in time what is better.[2]

Sceptical of the claims of those who professed to declare the nature and character of deity, in terms reminiscent of the Buddha, he said:

> There never was nor will be a man who has certain knowledge about the gods. . . . Even if he should chance to say the complete truth, yet he himself knows not that it is so.[3]

Thus with a degree of speculative freedom unknown in Mesopotamian and Egyptian cultures the Indo-European mind was now questioning accepted principles and beliefs. The most searching inquiries were made into the nature of religious traditions, in precisely that aspect of life which the Mesopotamians and Egyptians regarded as inviolable and sacrosanct and as accessible to the priests alone. This new spirit of inquiry was not, however, negative or subversive in its effects. Rather, inaugurating the age of reason it led to a positive and scientific attitude to life, while the superstitions and obscurantism of the Mesopotamians and Egyptians led to a despondency from which in vain they tried to escape by reflection on the past.

---

[1] Fragment 14 (Burnet, ibid.).
[2] Fragment 18 (Burnet, ibid.).
[3] Fragment 34 (Burnet, op. cit., p. 121).

III

THE VOICE OF ISRAEL

IN an age of such rapid and revolutionary change as that which
marked the collapse of the great empires of Assyria and Egypt
and which witnessed the rise to world significance of the
peoples of Persia and Greece it is important to consider how
Israel accepted and interpreted the issue of these events. For Israel
as a nation was not detached from the vicissitudes of these event-
ful years. Since the time of Sargon II Samaria had been incorporated into the Assyrian empire and from about 700 onwards
Judah had been a vassal of the Assyrian rulers. During the
following century therefore Assyrian influence was widely
exerted on Judah.[1] It was, however, in the sphere of religion
that the dominance of the conqueror was most bitterly experienced. For submission to the power of Assyria also involved
recognition of her gods. Thus, throughout the reign of Manasseh,
when Judah was reduced to a vassal state of Assyria, the recognition of Assyrian deities was an indispensable condition of
vassalage. However, then, Manasseh himself may have been
attracted by the form of Assyrian worship, it was in some measure
due to the political exigencies of the day that we read: 'He built
again the high places . . . and reared up altars for Baal, and made
an Asherah . . . and worshipped all the host of heaven and served
them . . . And he made his son to pass through the fire and
practised augury and used enchantments' (2 Kgs. 21: 3–6).

Such characteristically Assyrian religious practices introduced
into Israelite worship appear to have involved Manasseh in open
conflict with many of his people. The Hebrew historian reports
that Manasseh 'shed innocent blood very much' (2 Kgs. 21: 16),

---

[1] Cf. G. Hölscher, *Die Profeten*, Leipzig, 1914, pp. 261–264.

and it is likely that he was concerned only with establishing the innocence of the religious beliefs of those who suffered.[1] That there was, however, a considerable element of the nation which continued to practise the ideals of Yahwism may be seen from the support which was later accorded the reforms of Josiah. Whatever the provenance of the document which inspired this reform it seems that in accordance with its injunctions Josiah destroyed the idols and objects of Assyrian worship which Manasseh had introduced into the temple: 'And the king commanded . . . to bring forth out of the temple of Yahweh all the vessels that were made for Baal, and for Asherah, and for all the host of heaven, and he buried them without Jerusalem' (2 Kgs. 23 : 4). But the actions of Josiah were not confined to cleansing the temple of idolatrous objects. He contemplated a reform on a national scale, and 'defiled the high places where the priests had burned incense, from Gaza to Beersheba' (2 Kgs. 23 : 8). He further visualised a centralisation of worship, for we are told, 'He brought all the priests out of the cities of Judah' (ibid.). That the cleansed altar in Jerusalem was intended to be the centre of this worship is evident from the further comment: 'Nevertheless, the priests of the high places did not come up to the altar of Yahweh in Jerusalem, but they ate unleavened bread among their brethren' (2 Kgs. 23 : 9). These measures of reform undertaken by Josiah in accordance with the directions of the recently acquired law-book are so much in agreement with the injunctions of Deuteronomy, chapters 12–18, that, apart from other considerations, it is highly probable that this law-book underlies at least these chapters in the present book of Deuteronomy.[2]

---

[1] Cf. A. C. Welch, *Jeremiah, His Time and His Work* (reprinted 1951), p. 6; also J. A. Montgomery, 'Kings,' I.C.C., 1951 (ed. H. S. Gehman), p. 251.

[2] Cf. here J. P. Hyatt, 'Jeremiah and Deuteronomy', J.N.E.S., 1, 1942, pp. 158–159; J. Skinner, *Prophecy and Religion*, 6th impress., Camb., 1948, p. 91; R. H. Pfeiffer, *Intro. to the Old Test.*, p. 181. For the various views on the origin and date of Deuteronomy the following works may be consulted: *The Problem of Deuteronomy: A Symposium*, by J. A. Bewer, L. B. Paton, G. Dahl in J.B.L., 47, 1928, pp. 305–379; A. R. Siebens, *L'Origine du Code Deutéronomique*, Paris, 1929; R. H. Pfeiffer, *The History, Religion and Literature of Israel*, in H.T.R., 27, 1934, pp. 308 ff.; W. A. Irwin, *An Objective Criterion for the Dating of Deuteronomy*, A.J.S.L., 56, 1939, pp. 337–349; C. R. North, *Pentateuchal Criticism, in The Old Testament and Modern Study* (ed. Rowley), 1951, pp. 48–52. For the

Josiah's reforms were undertaken as a reactionary measure against Assyrian influences and Canaanite survivals, and, in demanding conformity to a definite standard of worship, attempted to regulate the practice of Hebrew religion. Our historical documents are, however, silent on the state of religion in Judah after the reforms, nor do they give any indication as to how the religious and national leaders regarded the political situation which changed so rapidly after the battle of Megiddo. It is therefore to the contemporary prophetic voice that we must turn for a study of the history and religion of Israel during the critical years which followed the death of Josiah. For the prophets were the channels through which the voice of God was interpreted and articulated in Israel; and it is significant that the classical age of prophecy coincides with the most troublous days of her history.

According to the biblical evidence the prophets were the chief agents of divine revelation. Thus, in the book of Hosea Yahweh is represented as saying: 'I spoke to the prophets; it was I who multiplied visions, and through the prophets gave parables' (12: 10, R.S.V.). Amos reminded his hearers that 'the Lord God does nothing without revealing his secret to his servants the prophets' (3: 7, R.S.V.). The writer of 2 Kgs. 17: 13, remarked that 'Yahweh warned Israel and Judah by every prophet'; while at a later date a New Testament writer tells us that 'In many and various ways God spoke of old to our fathers by the prophets' (Heb. 1: 1, R.S.V.). It is customary to apply the term 'ecstasy' to the media through which the prophet receives and delivers his message,[1] and some scholars further attempt to explain this particular experience in terms of modern psychology.[2] Unanimity,

view that more than one code is to be discerned in the present text of Deut. 12–18 see the analysis by C. A. Simpson, 'A Study of Deuteronomy 12–18', in A.T.R., 34, 1952, pp. 247–251.

[1] E.g., Hölscher, *Die Profeten*, pp. 1–77; T. H. Robinson, T.R., N.F., 3, 1931, pp. 75–101; cf. also O. Eissfeldt, 'The Prophetic Literature', in *The Old Testament and Modern Study*, pp. 134–145.

[2] E.g., G. Widengren, *Literary and Psychological Aspects of the Hebrew Prophets*, Uppsala, 1948, pp. 94–120; also H. Wheeler Robinson, 'Hebrew Psychology', in *The People and the Book* (ed. Peake), Oxford, 1925, pp. 353–382, and *Inspiration and Revelation in the Old Testament*, pp. 172–186.

however, has not been reached as to what extent 'ecstasy' or
any such psychic experience was a characteristic of the true
prophet.[1] And it may be doubted if the term 'ecstasy', deriving
as it does from a Greek concept of personality, adequately
expresses the presuppositions of Hebrew psychology.[2] It is, moreover, probable that no one kind of mental experience is sufficient
to account for the phenomena which contributed to the prophetic
consciousness, but that its constituents were as manifold and
complex as the 'many and various ways' mentioned by the author
of Hebrews. But whatever the precise media through which God
communicated his will to 'his servants the prophets' such prophets 'stood in the council of Yahweh to perceive and hear his
word' (Jer. 23 : 18).   These prophets in their turn transmitted to
the people of their day the contents of the divine message in clear
and unmistakable language.[3]

But the function of the prophet was not limited to that of mere
prediction. For the prophets were not content with declaring what
Yahweh would bring to pass. They closely identified themselves
with the people to whom they prophesied and tried to influence
the fortunes of their country. The professional prophet, offering
his service in so far as it was a means of livelihood, regarded his
duties discharged when he delivered his oracle (Amos 7: 12;
Micah 3: 5, 11; Ezek. 22: 28).   But the genuine prophet of
Yahweh did not thus detach himself from the implicates of his
message. He may have had to deliver a prophecy of doom because
of the unrighteousness of the nation, but he was also prepared to
share in the consequences of that unrighteousness. Again, the

[1] Cf., e.g., S. Mowinckel, 'The "Spirit" and the "Word" in the Pre-exilic Reforming
Prophets', J.B.L., 53, 1934, pp. 199–227, in which he recognises certain psychical distinctions in the experience of the true and false prophets.

[2] H. W. Robinson, *Inspiration and Revelation in the Old Testament*, p. 180, who thought
that ' "Possession" or some other term denoting invasion is preferable to the commonly
used "ecstasy".'

[3] 'Prophecy at its height was not a psychological phenomenon with psychological
criteria: it was the sanity of the prophets and not their manticism that made them such
tremendous factors in human history.' (S. A. Cook, *The Old Testament, A Reinterpretation*,
Camb., 1936, p. 189.) Similarly, speaking of the authority of the prophets, W. A. Irwin
remarked: 'It is important that we recognise the course of serious thinking entailed
before they dared appear in public to announce themselves religious leaders.' (*The Old
Testament: Keystone of Human Culture*, New York, 1952, p. 48.)

calling of the true prophet was not one chosen by himself. On the contrary, prophecy was a burden which all the great prophets only assumed with reluctance. Isaiah (6: 5) expressed his utter unworthiness to be the mouthpiece of Yahweh: Amos (7: 14) declared that his natural aptitude was that of a shepherd and vine-dresser: Jeremiah (1: 6) pleaded his youthfulness as a token of his inability to undertake the work of a prophet. But it was futile to protest, for when 'The Lord God hath spoken who can but prophesy' (Amos 3: 8). As Yahweh took Amos 'from following the flock' (Amos 7: 15), so He cleansed Isaiah of his alleged impurities and commanded him 'Go and tell this people' (Is. 6: 9). In like manner He assured Jeremiah of his calling, saying: 'To whomsoever I shall send thee thou shalt go, and whatsoever I shall command thee thou shalt speak' (Jer. 1: 7). There could be no resisting this word of Yahweh which, having invaded the personalities of the prophets, demanded expression through them. Because of the divine source of his message and of the prophet's close association with his people we naturally find the voice of the prophet expressed most clearly in the critical periods of Israel's history. Isaiah, Amos, and Hosea all thus spoke; and therefore the importance and relevance of Jeremiah for a discussion of the period immediately under consideration becomes at once apparent.[1] The book of Jeremiah is not, however, arranged in chronological order, nor indeed can it be maintained that all the oracles and material which it embodies were composed by the prophet himself. In common with all the prophetic literature of the Old Testament many sources, with numerous editorial additions, combine to form the present book.[2] Yet when studied against the

[1] The oracles of the contemporary prophets, Nahum, Habbakuk, and Zephaniah also, of course, provide information regarding the international situation of their day: e.g., Nahum 3; Hab. 1; Zeph. 2: 12-15. See C. V. Pilcher, *Three Hebrew Prophets and the Passing of the Empires*, Lond., 1913.

[2] Cf. Oesterley and Robinson, *Introd. to the Books of the Old Test.*, pp. 290-307; R. H. Pfeiffer, *Introd. to the Old Test.*, pp. 482-511; J. A. Bewer, *The Book of Jeremiah*, vol. 1, Lond., 1951, pp. 9-10; W. Rudolph, 'Jeremía', H.A.T., Tübingen, 1947, pp. xiii-xix; John Bright, 'The Date of the Prose Sermons of Jeremiah', J.B.L., 70, 1951, pp. 14-29; also H. G. May, 'Towards an Objective Approach to the Book of Jeremiah, in J.B.L., 61, 1942, pp. 139-153, for the view that the material of Jeremiah was first compiled in book form as late as the fifth century B.C.

3

background of known events, it will not only be found to supplement our historical sources, but will disclose the special significance of the teaching of Jeremiah for the Israelites of his day.

Jeremiah may justly be regarded as one of the greatest of our biblical figures, and as one of the most significant in the whole history of religious thought. He was born in the little village of Anathoth some few miles north of Jerusalem.[1] He was still but a youth of scarcely twenty years old when he was called to the prophetic office (1 : 6; 16 : 2). Tradition ascribes his call to 'the thirteenth year' of Josiah's reign (1 : 2), that is, in 626 B.C. Mention is also made in other places in the book to his activity in the reign of Josiah: these are, 1 : 2; 3 : 6; 25 : 3; and 36 : 2. The authenticity of these passages has, however, long been open to question,[2] and among recent scholars J. P. Hyatt has convincingly argued that they are insertions of a later editor who wished to claim for the Deuteronomic code the sanction of the great prophet.[3] Believing that the fall of Ashur was the signal for Jeremiah's call Hyatt places the beginning of his ministry within the years 614–612.[4] Accepting many of Hyatt's arguments H. G. May contends that much of the undated oracular material in chapters 1–25 of the book can be placed in the reign of Jehoiakim and accordingly concludes that Jeremiah did not begin his ministry till after the death of Josiah,[5] a position already reached by Horst in 1923.[6] More recently, from a consideration of chapter 36 alone, C. A. Simpson reached the same conclusion. Professor Simpson notes that the prophecies dictated there by Jeremiah to Baruch comprised 'all the words' which Yahweh had himself 'spoken' to Jeremiah since the beginning of his ministry. The ultimate purpose

[1] Jer. 1 : 1; Anathoth is accepted by most scholars as the place of the prophet's birth, although Jerusalem has been suggested by some; e.g., T. J. Meek, *Expositor*, 25, 1925, pp. 215–222.

[2] Cf. H. Winckler, *Geschichte Israels*, Leipzig, 1899, 1, pp. 112 f., who placed the prophet's call in 610; A. F. Puukko, *Jeremias Stellung zum Deuteronomium* (Alttest. Studien für R. Kittel, 1913), pp. 126–153.

[3] J.B.L., 59, 1940, pp. 511–513; J.N.E.S., 1, 1942, p. 166.

[4] J.B.L., 59, 1940, pp. 499–513. He recently wrote, however, 'The earliest messages of Jeremiah were delivered in the reign of Jehoiakim,', *Interpreter's Bible*, V, 1956, p. 780.

[5] J.B.L., 61, 1942, 147 ff.; J.N.E.S., 4, 1945, pp. 217–227.

[6] Z.A.W., 41, 1923, pp. 94–153.

of the dictation of the prophecies, and their compilation into a scroll, was that they should reach the ears of Jehoiakim. The oracles were first read in the temple (36: 10) but, having received news of their content, the princes and officials demanded that they should also be read in their own presence (36: 15). On hearing them they were so concerned that they 'turned one to another in fear' (36: 16) and judged their contents of such importance as to decide that they should be brought to the notice of the king. Jehoiakim, who since his accession in 608 had heard Jeremiah's warnings, was now little disposed to be reminded of them and after listening to but a few pages threw the oracles into the fire (36: 20–23). The circumstances of the occasion, however, explain both the king's anger and the purpose of Jeremiah in arranging that the oracles should be brought to his attention once more. For the battle of Carchemish had just been decided and it was evident that the victorious Chaldeans would sooner or later turn their attention towards Judah unless Jehoiakim desisted from pursuing a course which committed him to the full implications of the foreign policy of Egypt (cf. 2: 18, 36–37). The oracles which comprised all that Jeremiah had uttered up to that date must therefore have been directly relevant to the crisis which had developed on the rout of the Egyptians at Carchemish (605); and only oracles delivered since Jehoiakim became the vassal of Necho could have had an immediate bearing on the situation. Professor Simpson thus concludes: 'This would seem to suggest that Jeremiah's ministry had begun in 608, the year of Josiah's death at Megiddo and of the subjection of Judah to Egyptian suzerainty.'[1] The cogency of this argument and the association between king and prophet which it recognises is further attested by the consideration that while we know of no association between Jeremiah and Josiah we can point to serious efforts on Jeremiah's part to influence the policies of Jehoiakim and Zedekiah (cf. e.g., 26: 21; 36; 37: 17–21; 38: 14 f.). Indeed Jeremiah maintained as close an association with these two kings as did Isaiah

---

[1] *Jeremiah: The Prophet of 'My People'*, Winslow Memorial Lecture, 1947 (Seabury-Western Theological Seminary, Evanston, Illinois, 1947), pp. 7–10 (quotation from page 10).

with Ahaz and Hezekiah and thus may be said to continue the relationship between king and prophet which obtained since the time of Nathan (1 Kgs. 1).

As Jeremiah's commission is connected with a prediction of the coming of the foe from the north (1 : 13 f.) an attempt to identify this foe is essential to determining the date of his call. The foe is to be the instrument of Yahweh's judgment on Judah, and oracles relating to them appear throughout the early chapters of the book (e.g., 1 : 13–16; chs. 4–6; 8 : 14–17; 10 : 18–22). Since the time of Eichhorn most critics have interpreted these oracles as referring to a Scythian invasion of Palestine which Jeremiah is thought to have expected after his call.[1] Scholars who thus argue assume that Jeremiah began his ministry in 626, but even so, as Wilke pointed out,[2] there are many difficulties in the way of this interpretation. There is no evidence for a Scythian invasion of Palestine at any time except for a reference in Herodotus. This writer says that in overcoming the Medes 'the Scythians became master of all Asia. From thence they proceeded to Egypt, and when they reached Palestine in Syria, Psammetichus, King of Egypt, having met them with presents and prayers, diverted them from advancing further.... For twenty-eight years, then, the Scythians governed Asia' (1, 104–106). In Book 4, 1, however, Herodotus confines the activity and dominion of the Scythians to Upper Asia, that is, to the Iranian plateau.[3] We there read: 'For the Scythians, as I have before mentioned (1, 106) ruled over Upper Asia for eight-and-twenty years. For while in pursuit of the Cimmerians, they entered Asia, and overthrew the empire of the Medes; for these last, before the arrival of the Scythians, ruled over Asia. Those Scythians, however, after they had been abroad eight-and-twenty years, and returned to their own country, after

---

[1] See A. Condamin, *Le Livre de Jérémie*, Paris, 3rd edn., 1936, pp. 61 f., for an account of the history of the exegesis of these oracles. Duhm referred to them as the 'Scythian Songs' (*Das Buch Jeremia*, Leipzig, 1901, pp. 48 ff.). Of later scholars who favoured this interpretation the following may be mentioned: Hölscher, op. cit., pp. 272–278; Skinner, op. cit., pp. 34–35; J. A. Bewer, op. cit., 1, p. 21; T. H. Robinson, *A History of Israel*, 3rd impress., 1951, pp. 413 f.

[2] *Das Skythenproblem im Jeremia Buch* (Alttest. Studien für R. Kittel, 1913), pp. 222–254.

[3] A. T. Olmstead, *The History of the Persian Empire*, Chicago, 1948, p. 32, n. 87.

such an interval, a task no less than the invasion of Media awaited.'
An incursion into Media therefore seems to have been the extent
of their invasions. The Egyptian king mentioned in 1, 105 could
have been Psammetichus I (663–609). But it may be doubted if
this able ruler who founded the twenty-sixth dynasty and who
on his accession expelled the Assyrians from Egypt, would have
negotiated with the Scythians in the manner described by
Herodotus. There is no indication as to what period the twenty-
eight years mentioned in both passages cover. Herodotus does
mention, however, that having subdued the Scythians, the Medes
'reduced the Assyrians into subjection' and further that 'Cyaxares
died after he had reigned forty years, including the time of the
Scythian dominion' (1, 106). Cyaxares, who came to the throne
in 653,[1] launched his attack on the Assyrians in 614[2] so that
the Scythians must have been subdued by 615 at the latest. The
beginning of a twenty-eight-year period of Scythian domination
would therefore fall in about 643. Now Herodotus says that it
was on the defeat of the Medes that the Scythians turned south-
wards (1, 104–5) so that their invasion of Palestine would have
been shortly after 643. But at this time Ashurbanipal's strong hand
exercised authority over all the Palestinian states[3] and Judah which
had been a vassal of the empire since 700 was still protected by it.
It is therefore questionable if the Scythians could have invaded
Palestine in about 643. But even if the reference in Herodotus
rests on some historical basis and we are to believe that the
Scythian raiders then penetrated as far as Palestine it is still
difficult to see how such raids could have aroused Jeremiah to
prophesy some seventeen years later. For there is again no evidence
that the Scythians were in Palestine in 626 or that they appeared
there shortly afterwards.[4] Indeed failing to verify that the

---

[1] A. T. Olmstead, op. cit., p. 31.

[2] C. J. Gadd, *The Fall of Nineveh*, pp. 9 and 25.   [3] A.N.E.T., p. 294.

[4] C.f., e.g., Skinner who remarked: 'The opening of Jeremiah's ministry . . . coincides
approximately with the death of Ashurbanipal, and therefore with the two earliest
attacks of the Medes on Nineveh, first under Phraortes and then, shortly afterwards, under
his son Cyaxares' (op. cit., pp. 38–39). But Phraortes died in 653 and was succeeded by
his son the same year. Nor can the apocalyptic nature of the description of the coming of
the day of Yahweh in Zephaniah I be accepted as historical evidence for the appearance
of the Scythians around 626. Indeed 2: 13–15 presupposes the fall of Nineveh in 612.

Scythians or any other hostile people were in Palestine around 626 some scholars resorted to the expedient of saying that Jeremiah began his ministry expecting a Scythian invasion but when it did not materialise he subsequently modified his oracles to make them applicable to the Chaldeans.[1] This view, however, scarcely does justice to the inexorable nature of the divine message which it was the prophet's task to deliver. Consequently, recognising the untenability of this position, others abandoned the Scythian theory and attributing the oracles in question to the latter part of the prophet's ministry identified the foe with the Chaldeans. This was the course adopted by Wilke. For this, however, he was criticised by Welch, who, holding that the oracles belong to the beginning of Jeremiah's ministry, remarked, 'Wilke's solution only brings with it fresh difficulties'.[2] Welch himself interpreted the foe from the north eschatologically, and saw in the term not a reference to a geographical enemy but, rather, 'the proclamation of the coming judgment of God on a sinful world'.[3] Although placing Jeremiah's oracles about the foe from the north within the years 626–624 Volz did not see in them a reference to the Scythians, nor indeed to any 'definite enemy which may be politically distinguished'. Rather, having 'received from Yahweh the message that a military power is breaking in from the north' Jeremiah 'knows no more and desires to know no more'.[4] Yet the urgency with which Jeremiah spoke and the description of the enemy which he gives, suggest that he referred to a definite enemy which may be politically distinguished. Of course those scholars who think that he was provoked to prophesy on the fall of Ashur naturally associate the Medes with the foe. Hence, placing Jeremiah's call within the period 614–612 Hyatt

---

[1] E.g., Pfeiffer, *Intro. to the Old Test.*, pp. 494–495; J. A. Bewer, op. cit., p. 21.

[2] Op. cit., p. 104.

[3] Op. cit., p. 110. W. A. L. Elmslie, however, 'considers' Welch's argument 'to be generally valid' (*How Came Our Faith*, Camb., 1948, p. 314, n. 1). More novel is the suggestion of Alfred Haldar who thinks that Jeremiah is drawing from the ideas and vocabulary of the Babylonian New Year Festival and that the foe from the north is a reference to the sham fight enacted at that festival (*Associations of Cult Prophets among the Ancient Semites*, Uppsala, 1945, pp. 157 ff.).

[4] *Der Prophet Jeremia* (H.A.T.), Leipzig, 1922, p. 58.

claimed that 'the foe from the north is to be identified with the Chaldeans and their allies'.[1] This would assign the first years of the prophet's activity to the reign of Josiah. Yet it is questionable if the situation as depicted in the oracles themselves, and in the material in the early part of the book, accords with the reign of Josiah. Thus in chapter 4 where the coming devastation of the land is in consequence of the people's idolatry, we read that 'the heart of the king shall perish' (v. 9). This implies that the king was also guilty of the sins committed by the nation; yet in 22 : 15–16 Josiah is commended for the justice and righteousness which he practised during his reign. On the other hand Jeremiah speaks of Jehoiakim in derogatory terms in 22 : 18–19, while his denunciation of him is also to be seen in 8 : 1 f. (cf. also 36 : 30–31). Further, the political circumstances suggested by certain references in chapter 2 can scarcely be associated with the reign of Josiah : 'And now what do you gain by going to Egypt, to drink the waters of the Euphrates? . . . How lightly you gad about, changing your way! You shall be put to shame by Egypt as you were put to shame by Assyria' (vv. 18, 36; cf. also v. 16). The relevance of these passages to the reign of Jehoiakim is obvious when it is remembered that on his accession he became the vassal of Egypt and that he later manifested pro-Egyptian sympathies regardless of the power of Babylon (2 Kgs. 23 : 34–35; 24 : 1). But the potential danger emanating from that power was tremendous. For the failure of the Assyrians and Egyptians to regain control of Harran in 609[2] indicated that in the near future the Chaldeans would wield dominion over all the nations of the Near East. And if A. B. Davidson was correct in assuming that 'prophecies were suggested by some great movement among the nations in which Jehovah's presence is already felt'[3] then Jeremiah was confronted with circumstances before which no genuine prophet could remain silent. Already 'in the beginning of the

---

[1] J.B.L., 59, 1940, p. 509.   [2] C. J. Gadd, *The Fall of Nineveh*, p. 26.
[3] *Nahum, Habakkuk and Zephaniah* (Camb. Bible for Schools), 1899, p. 282. Similarly S. A. Cook remarked that the prophets 'are great, not only because of their deep insight into the profounder factors that make history, but because their survey of events is not confined to their own country' (*The Old Testament, A Reinterpretation*, p. 171).

reign of Jehoiakim' (26: 1) it was evident to his prophetic
eye that 'a great nation is stirring' (6: 22) and that for Judah 'evil
looms out of the north' (6: 1). Unless Jehoiakim were to change
his policy the Judeans would experience 'sword' and 'famine'
(5: 12), their 'fenced cities' would be demolished and they
themselves would 'serve strangers in a land' not theirs (5: 19).
As yet it would be unwise for Jeremiah to disclose the identity
of these 'strangers'. He could intimate to Jehoiakim (ch. 36) the
danger threatening from the north without, perhaps, referring to
the Chaldeans by name,[1] but indiscreet mention of them while
Judah was a vassal of Egypt would provoke dangerous opposition
from members of the state who were Egyptian in sympathy.
It is significant, however, that when Nebuchadrezzar subdued
Jerusalem in 597 and enthroned Zedekiah as a vassal of Babylon
(2 Kgs. 24: 17) the enemy is henceforth referred to by name.
Shortly before the second Chaldean onslaught against Jerusalem
in 586 we hear the prophet saying: 'Thus saith Yahweh: Behold,
I am giving this city into the hand of the Chaldeans and into the
hand of Nebuchadrezzar king of Babylon, and he shall take it.
The Chaldeans who are fighting against this city shall come and
set this city on fire, and burn it ...' (32: 28–29). Similarly in
34: 2 we read: 'Thus saith Yahweh ... Go and speak to Zedekiah
king of Judah and say to him, Thus saith Yahweh ... Behold, I
am giving this city into the hand of the king of Babylon, and he
shall burn it with fire.' Jeremiah would have had little to fear
from the Babylonians in proclaiming such a message, while he
could now more than ever count on the protection of the in-
fluential house of Shaphan (cf. 26: 24) which was favourable to
Babylonian suzerainty.[2] It seems, then, that the foe from the north
was a term which Jeremiah applied to the Chaldeans when they
were looming on the horizon as potential enemies of Judah and

[1] Babylon is mentioned in verse 29 and also in 20: 4, but these verses are very probably
secondary (cf. H. G. May, 'The Chronology of Jeremiah's Oracles', J.N.E.S., 4, 1945,
pp. 224 and 226).
[2] That the house of Shaphan was pro-Babylonian may be inferred from the fact that
on the fall of Jerusalem in 586 Nebuchadrezzar 'made Gedaliah the son of Ahikam, the
son of Shaphan, governor' (2 Kgs. 25: 22).

that he referred to the enemy by name after their invasion of the land in 597.

The question as to how Jeremiah regarded the Deuteronomic law has always presented problems. If he began his career in 626 we should expect to hear of his association with the promulgation of this law five years later. The biblical evidence, however, in no way connects him with it. Indeed in the present arrangement of the book[1] much obscurity attaches to Jeremiah from 'the thirteenth year' of Josiah (1:2) until 'the beginning of the reign of Jehoiakim (26:1) when we find the first dated oracle since his call. This obscurity has been explained by assuming that Jeremiah approved of the Deuteronomic Law during the early years of its publication but that on its obvious failure to meet the spiritual needs of the people on the death of Josiah he resumed an active ministry.[2] On the basis of 11:1-8 it has also been suggested that Jeremiah was actually an advocate of Deuteronomy,[3] while the opposition he experienced from his own kinsmen (12:6) is interpreted as arising from his support of the centralisation of sacrifice at the altar of Jerusalem thereby depriving his brethren of their office at the local shrine.[4] Yet this view of the prophet as approving and disapproving of the same law represents him as an unstable and changeable character and is based on an uncritical reading of the text. It is strange that Jeremiah who appears to have had close contact with Jehoiakim and Zedekiah should nowhere have any association with Josiah. If he had been prophesying in 621 we would expect to find some record of Josiah consulting him on the matter of the publication of the law-book instead of the otherwise unknown Huldah the prophetess. And this silence is all the more remarkable when we recall that

[1] 'In many cases we have nothing but brief fragments, whose original context it is impossible to guess, and these have been flung together almost haphazard, by some collectors' (Oesterley and Robinson, *Intro. to the Books of the Old Test.*, p. 298; see also H. G. May, 'The Chronology of Jeremiah's Oracles', J.N.E.S., 4, 1945, pp. 217–227).

[2] E.g., Skinner, op. cit., pp. 89–108; Rudolph, op. cit., p. 69; Bewer, op. cit., p. 6; cf. also H. H. Rowley, 'The Prophet Jeremiah and the Book of Deuteronomy', in *Studies in Old Testament Prophecy*, p. 174.

[3] Skinner, op. cit., pp. 97–102; Rowley, ibid., 172 f.; Bewer, op. cit., p. 43.

[4] Skinner, op. cit., p. 109 f.; Rowley, ibid., p. 173.

Ahiakim, a prominent member of the royal household, who later
befriended Jeremiah (26: 24) was one of the delegates who visited
her on the occasion (2 Kgs. 22: 14). Nor can it be that Jeremiah
would have disapproved of associating with the king, for he is
known to have spoken favourably of him (22: 15–16). He need
not, however, have been prophesying during Josiah's reign to
have known of his honourable qualities. The covenant which
Jeremiah is represented as commending to the observance of the
people in 11: 3–8 is, as the text stands, more likely to have been
the Sinaitic covenant than the Deuteronomic law; but aside from
this consideration, Hyatt, on a detailed analysis of the passage, has
convincingly demonstrated its dependence on Deuteronomic
thought and phraseology and consequently its composition by
later Deuteronomic hands.[1] Nor is the theory of Jeremiah's early
support of the Deuteronomic Law the only or most natural
explanation of his persecution by the men of Anathoth. For the
words of doom which the prophet spoke against the nation
would prove so embarrassing to his people that they would be
provoked into taking some measures to silence him.

It is thus only by adhering to the date of 626 for the call of
Jeremiah that the question of his relationship to Deuteronomy is
problematical. For in holding that date various expedients are
adopted in order to maintain that the prophet could not have
been indifferent to a law published five years after his call. When,
however, Jeremiah began his ministry the circumstances of the
publication of Deuteronomy had fallen into the background.
Josiah who sanctioned its publication was dead and the national
aspirations it fostered were suppressed by Egyptian suzerainty
and the impending threat of danger from Babylon. It is inherently
improbable that Jeremiah could have approved in principle of
Deuteronomy, for, while we have no definite evidence that he
specifically condemned it as such, he was engaged in constant

---

[1] J.N.E.S., I, 1942, pp. 168–170. Of course Duhm (*Das Buch Jeremia*, 1901, pp. 106–111)
and Cornill (*Das Buch Jeremia*, 1905, pp. 143–145) already questioned the authenticity of
the passage. Volz (op. cit., pp. 127–132) and Rudolph (op. cit., pp. 67–68) regard it as
composite.

conflict with the people of Judah who were influenced by its presuppositions.

The exercise of a ministry spent against a background of prophecies of doom was necessarily a difficult one. But the circumstances which obtained in Judah in Jeremiah's day tended to accentuate such difficulties. For up to Josiah's death the kingdom had been enjoying a period of political independence and its boundaries had been extended as far as Samaria (2 Kgs. 23 : 15–20). The Josianic reformation had, moreover, the effect of establishing Judah's religion on a firm and national basis. Subjection to Egypt was consequently all the more difficult to accept and many, doubtless, hoped that by one political move or another (cf. Jer. 2 : 16, 18–19, 36–37) they would eventually regain their independence. Jeremiah was therefore an unwelcome figure as he appeared prophesying a message of doom and condemning the religious practices of the people.

However much the Josianic reformation may have effected it is clear that in Jeremiah's day the ideals of the reformers were far from being realised. With obvious reference to the law of centralisation the writer of 2 Kgs. 23 : 9 remarked 'Nevertheless, the priests of the high places came not up to the altar of Yahweh in Jerusalem, but they ate unleavened bread among their brethren.' Much more serious for Jeremiah, however, was the opposition he experienced from the cult, or nationalist, prophets. Even the reformers were aware of the problem of prophetic utterances not inspired by Yahweh, for we read of instructions as to how such utterances should be accepted (Dt. 13 : 1–5) and also of the criterion whereby the predictions of a false prophet may be distinguished from those of the genuine prophet of Yahweh (Dt. 18 : 18–22). Unable to grasp the significance of contemporary political events these prophets advocated a nationalism which was entirely contrary to the policy entertained by Jeremiah. Wishing to find favour in the eyes of a nationalist public they represented Yahweh's message as 'It shall be well with you . . . No evil shall come upon you' (23 : 17). This was characteristic of the prophets whom Jeremiah denounced and with whom he was engaged in continuous conflict. Yahweh's judgment of them is: 'The prophets prophesy lies in my name: I sent them not, neither have I commanded them: they prophesy unto you a lying vision and divination, and a thing of nought and deceit of their own heart' (14: 14). They had not 'stood in the council of Yahweh to perceive and to hear his word' (23: 18); therefore their teaching is vain: 'they speak visions of their own minds, not from the mouth of Yahweh' (23: 16). Yahweh 'did not send the prophets, yet they ran'; He 'did not speak to them, yet they prophesied' (23: 21). Of course the prophetic members of a sanctuary which was recently established as the only legitimate one in the land would naturally exhibit an unusual degree of presumption. Hence, exalted by such an enhancement of their office, these prophets of Jerusalem regarded themselves superior to any former representatives of their profession, and especially to those who in earlier days prophesied in the now forgotten kingdom of Samaria. But while Yahweh could recall the folly of 'the prophets of Samaria' who prophesied by Baal (23: 13), He could also say 'In the prophets of Jerusalem I have seen a horrible thing' (23: 14). Indeed 'from the prophets of Jerusalem ungodliness has gone forth into all the land' (23: 15). Interested only in the professional aspect of their office and wishing to maintain that office 'by their lies and their recklessness' they do not 'profit' the 'people at all' (23: 32). Not commissioned by Yahweh, they lacked the originality of the true prophet and vied with one another as to the content of their message (23: 30). Confronting a leading one of these prophets with the charge of insincerity and falseness Jeremiah said: '. . . Hananiah, Yahweh has not sent you, but you have made this people trust in a lie' (28: 15).

The prophets were not, however, alone in their presentation of the belief of the assured presence of Yahweh and of His abiding protection for Israel. For the priests, with whom the prophets appear to be closely associated, also shared responsibility with the prophets in circulating messages of optimism and in engendering a spirit of national complacency. Of course the renovation of the temple and the official limitation of sacrifice to the altar at

Jerusalem enhanced the office of priesthood more than any other representative of the cultus; and it is therefore not surprising that the priests should now display a certain arrogance and assume a new sense of importance in the performance of their duties. They were also probably the custodians of the recently published code (cf. Jer. 2: 8), and this extension of their priestly functions would invest them with novel authority and significance in the eyes of the nation. Accordingly, both priest and prophet alike are now denounced by Jeremiah. He observes the priests supporting the policy of the prophets, and remarks that 'an appalling and horrible thing has happened in the land: the prophets prophesy falsely, and the priests rule at their direction' (5: 30-31). The moral standards of priest and prophet are no higher than those of the ordinary people, and both do little to allay the fears of those who seek guidance at their hands (6: 14). In the days of Hosea it was 'like people, like priest' (Hos. 4: 9), but now 'from prophet to priest every one deals falsely' (6: 13). 'Both prophet and priest are ungodly' and even in the house of God 'their wickedness' is found (23: 11). Nor is it likely that the ideal of sacrifice at one altar was ever attained. We have already noted that 2 Kgs. 23: 9 preserves for us evidence to the effect that many rural priests did not conform to the Josianic regulations regarding sacrifice. But Jeremiah further informs us that even within the environs of Jerusalem not only was incense offered to heathen gods but that human sacrifice was made to Baal (19: 4-5). The priests, however, seem to have condoned these practices, for, when Jeremiah predicted the doom which would overtake the nation for this idolatry (19: 6-14) Pashhur, one of the leading Jerusalem priests, 'beat' him 'and put him in the stocks' (20: 1-2). Indeed the priests no less than the prophets were his avowed enemies (26: 11) and were amongst those who constituted 'the burden of Yahweh' (23: 33 with LXX).

But the most lamentable consequence of this conduct of the priests and prophets was that 'the people loved to have it so' (5: 31). For of course they gladly accepted pronouncements which assured them that all augured well for the future. Moreover, despite Egyptian suzerainty, the people of Jerusalem were rather disposed to think that their standard of religion left nothing to be desired. For was not the temple recently declared the only legitimate sanctuary at which sacrifice could be offered? Were not its priests and prophets thereby acclaimed superior to any in the land? Should not then their ministrations and pronouncements be regarded as expressing the will and authority of Yahweh himself? What indeed more natural than that the populace should say, 'for the law shall not perish from the priest . . . nor the word from the prophet'? (18: 18).

Jeremiah had not only a different opinion of their priests and prophets but also differed from them in his estimate of the validity of the sacrifices they made to Yahweh. He was not of course the first of the pre-exilic prophets to condemn sacrifice. Amos (5: 21-25), Hosea (6: 6), and Isaiah (1: 11-15) were all unanimous in their denunciation of sacrifice as a means of approach to God. And a passage in Micah, although denied to the prophet himself, nevertheless testifies to an ideal of worship which is not expressed in terms of sacrifice: 'With what shall I come before Yahweh and bow myself before God on high? Shall I come before him with burnt offerings, with calves of a year old? Will Yahweh be pleased with thousands of rams . . . ? He has showed you, O man, what is good; and what does Yahweh require of you but to do justice, and to love mercy and to walk humbly with your God?' (Mic. 6: 8). Some modern writers maintain that the prophets were not condemning sacrifice as such, but rather the absence of penitence and sincerity on the part of the worshipper.[1] Yet it is significant that in all their references to sacrifice the great prophets never regarded it as of the essence of religion.[2] Even Samuel who himself sacrificed at the ancient sanctuaries is represented as saying: 'Behold to obey is better than sacrifice and to hearken

[1] Cf., e.g., H. H. Rowley, 'The Unity of the Old Testament', B.J.R.L., 29, 1945–1946, pp. 326 ff.; Wheeler Robinson, *Inspiration and Revelation in the Old Testament*, p. 22.

[2] Skinner, op. cit., p. 181. Cf. also the observations of F. V. Filson: 'No system of sacrifice and ritual could provide the instruction and stimulus needed for the mature knowledge of God. The Mosaic and prophetic streams were the distinctive elements of the religion of Israel and the Temple did not adequately express and cultivate them.' (Temple, 'Synagogue and Church', B.A., Dec. 1944, p. 77.)

than the fat of rams' (1 Sam. 15: 22). On the other hand we cannot be certain as to the extent the pre-exilic prophets conceived of worship in Israel apart from the sanctuary and its ritual. Since the time of Solomon the temple and its ritual was established as a national institution (1 Kgs. 7: 51–8: 5) with which the nation as a whole identified itself and expressed its worship of Yahweh. The day had not yet come when Israel was capable of worshipping Yahweh in a form devoid of all mundane intermediaries and when God could be conceived of as spirit and worshipped in spirit and in truth.

While then the temple and its cultic associations was the focal point of the nation's worship, its sacrifices and ceremonies were regarded as the normal channel of communication with Yahweh. But in the time of Jeremiah there was more reason than ever for thinking that the temple was the divinely appointed means of worship. For it was not only repaired and cleansed of foreign cults, but according to the terms of the Deuteronomic law was designated the only place at which sacrifice could be made, and in consequence assumed a new degree of veneration and inviolability in the eyes of the populace. Early in his career, however, Jeremiah could quote Yahweh as saying: 'To what purpose does frankincense come to me from Sheba, or sweet cane from a distant land? Your burnt offerings are not acceptable, nor your sacrifices pleasing to me' (6: 20). On another occasion Yahweh is also represented as saying: 'Add your burnt offerings to your sacrifices, and eat the flesh' (7: 21). For flesh was intended for human consumption, and it was but a waste of food to burn it to ashes on the false assumption that it would be acceptable to God. Rather, said Yahweh: 'In the day that I brought them out of the land of Egypt, I did not speak to your fathers or command them concerning burnt offerings and sacrifices. But this command I gave them, Obey my voice, and I will be your God and you shall be my people' (7: 22). That was the only service God demanded from man: 'vows and sacrificial flesh' (11: 15, R.S.V.) are no substitute for it.

But Jeremiah's condemnation of the mode and standards of

worship current in his own day was not confined to sacrifice. Nor
indeed was this in itself the worst element in the religious practices of the populace. In addition to the common worship of Baal
(7 : 9) Jeremiah witnessed scenes in 'the cities of Judah and in the
streets of Jerusalem' which he thus described: 'The children
gather wood, the fathers kindle fire, and the women knead dough,
to make cakes for the queen of heaven' (7 : 18). Ishtar, the
Assyrian goddess of love and fertility, introduced into Jerusalem
by Manasseh (2 Kgs. 21 : 3-7), is here referred to as the queen of
heaven. As she was thought to represent the astral planet, cakes
made in the form of stars were used in connection with her
worship.[1] Yet side by side with such observances and the immoral
practices arising out of them, there seemed to have been a regular
attendance at the temple. Such a state of religion in the nation
compelled Jeremiah to address the Judeans on the subject of the
temple and the worship conducted there. It was a festival occasion
for we read that all Judah had come to worship Yahweh (7 : 2).
As the people assembled in the temple precincts Jeremiah confronted them with an oracle which might be rendered thus: 'Do
not trust in lying words, saying, "the temple of Yahweh, the
temple of Yahweh, the temple of Yahweh". What! is it stealing,
murdering and committing adultery, and swearing falsely, and
sacrificing to Baal, and then come and stand before me in this
house and say "We are delivered", so that ye can do all these
abominations? Is it a den of robbers this house has become in your
eyes? Yea, I have seen, saith Yahweh. But go to my sanctuary
which is in Shiloh where I set my name originally and see what
I did to it because of the wickedness of my people. And now
because ye do all these things saith Yahweh, "I will do to the
house in which ye trust as I did to Shiloh: I will cast you from my
presence as I have cast all your brethren." '[2] Jeremiah's criticism of
the cultus was, therefore, more thorough-going than had ever
previously been expressed in Israel. For, while the pronounce-

---

[1] J. A. Bewer, op. cit., I, p. 32.
[2] The present M.T. contains, of course, much editorial material: see the present
writer, 'A Note on Jeremiah 7 : 4', J.T.S., V, I, 1954, pp. 57-59.

ments of his predecessors regarding the religious validity of
sacrifice were negative, their remarks never extended to the
temple. In accordance with the tenets of their teaching Jeremiah
had said that holocausts were but a waste of flesh and rather than
be unacceptable to God should be eaten by the people themselves; but now the temple wherein sacrifice was offered would
itself be abolished by Yahweh. In the thought of Jeremiah, then,
the question of the theological validity of sacrifice resolved itself
into the belief that sacrifice with its entire cultic associations was
a hindrance to the spiritual conception of God and to the true
worshipping of Him.

In declaring that Yahweh would destroy the temple, regarded
by the people as the only medium through which He could be
worshipped, Jeremiah in effect propounded a new conception of
God. The temple and its sacrifice localised the worship and the
presence of Yahweh. But implicit in all the theology of Jeremiah's
teaching, and particularly towards the end of his ministry, was
the notion that Yahweh could be worshipped beyond the national
boundaries of Israel. For Yahweh was a God of distant as well as of
local lands: His eye penetrates the most 'secret places', and His
presence fills both 'heaven and earth' (23: 23). Yahweh's omnipotence is, moreover, reflected in the wonders of nature. He made
the sea and the sea-coast; He controls the movements of the waves
He giveth rain in its season and maintains mankind by His bless-
ings of harvest (5: 21–24). And although we can scarcely attribute
to Jeremiah the formulation of the conception of God found in
chapter 10 of the book that bears his name, it was a true instinct
of an editor which placed these verses (10: 5–16)[1] amongst
Jeremiah's oracles, for they are but the theological expression of a
view of God which he preached against a background of a rapidly
changing and developing historical scene. As Jeremiah recognised
God's hand in the movements of the nations, and consequently
the universal scope of His dominion, he became more convinced
that a system of worship which localised the divine presence constituted a total misconception of the nature of deity. Yet the

---

[1] They are reminiscent of the thought and theology of Deutero-Isaiah.

4

effects of the Deuteronomic legislations seriously hindered Jeremiah in his attempt to expound his own conception of God. For the limitation of sacrifice to Jerusalem but served to associate Yahweh more closely with the national temple. In attempting, therefore, to correct the inadequacy of this notion he was driven to a rejection of the religious principles of the state. And by declaring that God would bring the temple to an end he not only struck at the roots of the religious beliefs and practices of the people, but also at any surviving hopes of the restoration of the Josianic state.

After the battle of Carchemish Jeremiah intensified his efforts of warning the nation of the coming doom. The final defeat of the Assyrians and the withdrawal of Egypt from Asia heralded the westward advance of the Chaldeans.[1] Nor was it long before the issue of events vindicated the reality of the situation conceived by the prophet. By the year 603–2 Nebuchadrezzar was in the west and brought all the Palestinian states, including Judah, under his control.[2] Jehoiakim, however, only remained subject to him 'three years; then he turned and rebelled against him' (2 Kgs. 24: 1). Accordingly Nebuchadrezzar returned to Judah and, subduing Jerusalem, deported many of its leading citizens. Henceforth Jeremiah advocated a policy of submission to Babylon. It was futile to resist this world power, and therefore it was better to surrender than to be annihilated. This was the will of Yahweh who Himself was on the side of the Chaldeans and would turn the weapons of the Judeans against themselves (21 : 4–5). The only hope of survival and life was to submit without a struggle (21 : 8–10). The nation and temple would perish, but Yahweh would preserve the essentials of religion.

But neither the Judeans in Jerusalem nor the captives in Babylon could see the situation as Jeremiah did. Those deported in 597 consisted largely of the national leaders with whom Jeremiah had so often remonstrated in vain. Now, however, in the land of the

---

[1] Cf. 2 Kgs. 24: 7; Jer. 46: 2.

[2] John Bright, B.A., 12, 2, 1949, p. 50. See, however, D. J. Wiseman, *Chronicles of Chaldean Kings* (626–556 B.C.), Lond., 1956, pp. 26, 30, for the view that Jehoiathim submitted to Nebuchadrezzar as early as 605.

exile they were to undergo an experience which had the most far-reaching consequences for their religion. Far removed from the temple and bereft of the means and ritual of sacrifice, they were gravely concerned with the question as to how they could worship Yahweh. The belief that 'burnt offering and sacrifice' (2 Kgs. 5: 17) could be made to Yahweh on Israelite soil only had been of long standing in Israel,[1] but the recent law demanding the centralisation of sacrifice at the altar in Jerusalem emphasised this national conception of religion. Consequently, like David of old each one could now say: 'They have driven me out this day that I should have no share in the heritage of Yahweh, saying, "Go serve other gods"' (1 Sam. 26: 19). And in bitterness of spirit we hear an exile as he sat 'by the waters of Babylon' crying, 'How shall we sing Yahweh's song in a foreign land?' (Ps. 137: 1, 4).

The exiles would not therefore quickly abandon the hope of returning to Jerusalem. And political developments in the west now strengthened such a hope. The accession of Psammetichus II in 594 to the Egyptian throne was interpreted by the western states as a challenge to the power of Babylon. Thus Edom, Moab, Ammon, Tyre, and Sidon made representations to Zedekiah with a view to a general insurrection against Nebuchadrezzar (Jer. 27: 2 f.). Influenced by such movements a false prophet of Jerusalem, Hananiah, circulated in that 'same year', 593, a rumour that Jehoiachin 'with all the captives of Judah' together with the temple vessels would be restored to Jerusalem within the space of two years (Jer. 28: 2–4). Taking advantage of such rumours the false prophets in Babylon uttered oracles of optimism amongst the exiles and encouraged them to expect an early return (Jer. 29: 8–9, 21–22, 24, 31). Moreover, the Jews in Jerusalem attached a degree of odium to the notion of captivity, and, interpreting the administrative promotion to which many of them now attained as an indication of divine favour, rashly proclaimed that the land was their possession (Ezek. 11: 15). Jeremiah then took the opportunity offered by the occasion of a gathering before

[3] Cf. 2 Kgs. 17: 26; Amos. 7: 17; Hosea 9: 3.

the temple to address them on this matter. His estimate of the relative value of the exiles and remanent Judeans was expressed in terms of a basket of good and a basket of bad figs (23 : 1–8). The good figs were 'very good' like the figs that are 'first ripe'; but the bad figs are so bad that 'they cannot be eaten'. As therefore the bad figs which failed to come to maturity cannot be eaten and are cast away, so the Judeans who failed to fulfil the divine purpose of their creation would also be rejected of God. The good figs on the other hand, being the first fruits of the season, were a promise of good things to come. So the exiles were now spiritually the first fruits of God's people, the heralds of His universal message to mankind. Of them Yahweh could say: 'I will set mine eyes upon them for good . . . I will give them an heart to know that I am Yahweh; and they shall be my people and I will be their God' (24 : 6–7). The exiles were not, however, disposed to accept their captivity as a promise of divine favour. Rather, influenced by the false optimism of their prophets, and by similar utterances current in Jerusalem, their attitude to Babylon was one of ill-will and revolt.

Jeremiah, who had watched the development of events in Jerusalem and Babylon with the greatest concern, was now obliged to address himself to the exiles. Through the agency of ambassadors whom Zedekiah was sending to Babylon he was able to send them a letter of personal advice (29 : 3). Bearing in mind their resentment to the land of their captivity and their obsession with the hope of an immediate return he said: 'Build houses and live in them; plant gardens and eat their produce. Take wives and have sons and daughters . . . multiply there, and do not decrease. But seek the welfare of the land[1] where I have sent you into exile, and pray to Yahweh on its behalf, for in its welfare you will find your welfare' (29 : 5–7). This seemed strange to the exiles. For they were not only to settle and content themselves in Babylon but to 'pray to Yahweh on its behalf'. Their immediate reaction must have been to wonder what power could Yahweh the God of Israel exercise over the land of Babylon. Surely He must be

[1] With LXX.

as impotent there as the land itself was distasteful to them. The suggestion that Yahweh was interested in the welfare of Babylon was contrary to all they had known of Him. Besides there was no lack of evidence in their environment to suggest that Babylon was the domain of other gods. The exiles must have consequently regarded the tenor of Jeremiah's letter as inconsistent with their own situation and as being motivated by political rather than religious considerations. Jeremiah was not, however, speaking from the standpoint of political expediency when he counselled that the exiles should identify themselves with the welfare of Babylon. He was primarily concerned to impart a positive spiritual message but he had first to impress upon them the advisability of accepting their physical environment. For novel as the implication appeared to the exiles, Babylon was part of the realms of Yahweh. In deporting the Judeans Nebuchadrezzar was but acting as Yahweh's servant (27: 6) and consequently events in Babylon, as elsewhere in the Near East (27: 6-9), were directly under Yahweh's control. Babylonian citizenship was therefore not inconsistent with loyalty to Yahweh, and in contributing to the good of that state the exiles would but further His purpose. In direct answer to the question as to how they could 'worship Yahweh in a foreign land' Jeremiah's message was: 'I know the plans I have for you, says Yahweh, plans for welfare and not for evil, to give you a future and a hope. Then you will call upon me and pray unto me, and I will hear you' (29: 11-12). The essence of his message here was that Yahweh may be found irrespective of land or place by those who seek Him with earnestness of spirit and purpose. He therefore expresses explicitly what he could only imply while his audience had access to the ritual of a national worship; for participation of worship in the temple tended to perpetuate the notion of a national God. Attempting to correct this limited conception of deity Jeremiah informed the exiles that the true worship of Yahweh was independent of sacrifice and temple or of any such external accessories. Indeed, as he had earlier declared in his address in the temple, the worship conducted there was far from acceptable to God. But now Yahweh discloses the conditions which alone are necessary to effect communion with Him: to the worshipper who approaches Him in the simplicity of personal prayer His assurance is, 'I will hear you.' Prophets previous to Jeremiah could represent Yahweh as saying, 'Seek me and live' (Amos 5: 4; cf. Hos. 5: 15), but Jeremiah was the first of the Hebrew prophets to declare that He could be worshipped wherever He was sought in sincerity of spirit. Not only in Jerusalem, but by the waters of the Euphrates and on the 'tells' of Babylon could the comfort of Yahweh be experienced by whoever sought Him with the whole heart. By thus preaching Jeremiah was the first in Israel to expound a doctrine of God which was later to find its fullest expression in Him who said, 'Neither' on mount Gerizim 'nor in Jerusalem' will men 'worship the Father ... the hour is coming ... when the true worshippers will worship the Father in spirit and truth, for such the Father seeks to worship him' (John 4: 21–23). Envisaging the rudiments of this ideal Jeremiah proclaimed that the worship of Yahweh was neither confined to temple nor ceremony nor limited to any territory. A citizen may have a nation but true religion has none. The world is the sphere of the religion of Yahweh.[1]

But those who reject the sensory approach to God as being crude and inadequate and conceive of Him in terms of spirit and universality are not thereby immune from disconcerting questions regarding His nature and power. When the mind refuses to identify God with a particular shrine or form of ritual and, transcending such notions, thinks of Him in relation to the world and the cosmic forces, then new and disquieting problems arise. By conforming to certain sacrificial rites Jeremiah's unthinking countrymen expressed, and it seems satisfied, their religious impulses. Jeremiah on the other hand not only conceived of God as One who should be worshipped in spirit, but as Lord of nature (5: 22–24) and as a just and righteous Being (11: 20; 12: 1; 22: 3). Yet his own experience of the world raised the question as to its consistency with the view that it was created and governed by an omnipotent and righteous Being. He was therefore, perhaps,

---

[1] Cf. R. Kittel, 'Great Men and Movements in Israel', E. T., Leipzig, 1925, p. 361.

the earliest biblical thinker to deal with the question of theodicy.[1] He acknowledges that God is righteous (12: 1) but continues: 'Yet would I plead my case before thee. Why does the way of the wicked prosper? Why do all who are treacherous thrive? Thou plantest them, and they take root; they grow and bring forth fruit' (12: 1–2). As far as he knows he is innocent and righteous himself (12: 3) yet he is the object of the schemings of hostile crowds (20: 10). Dubious as to the efficacy of his ministry, and reproachful of his own existence, he curses the day he was born (20: 14–18). In extremities of agony he is driven to ask God, 'Why is my pain unceasing, my wound incurable, refusing to be healed?' (15: 18). But the scepticism which raised such questions yielded to a conception of God as One who tries 'the heart and the mind' (11: 20), and who has power 'to save . . . and deliver' (15: 20). For while his thoughts, in surpassing the limited conception of deity characteristic of his day, ranged over such perplexing yet natural problems, his personal and intimate fellowship with God led him to regard these problems as ultimately deriving from human perversity. Perverseness sprung from the heart of man, for Yahweh had said: 'The heart is deceitful above all things, and desperately corrupt; who can understand it?' But while the human heart is inscrutable to man it is in Yahweh's power to 'search the mind and try the heart' and thus 'to give to every man according to his ways, according to the fruit of his doings' (17: 9–10). The preaching of Jeremiah was henceforth frequently directed against the obduracy of the human heart (e.g., 5: 25–27; 9: 6). This is likewise the cause of Judah's apostasy: holding 'fast deceit . . . no man repents of his wickedness'; rather, 'everyone turns to his own course like a horse plunging headlong into battle' (8: 5–6). Circumcision of the heart rather than the flesh is then necessary if man would earn the favour of Yahweh (4: 4).

But Israel exhibited a tendency towards disobedience and obstinacy throughout her past history. God's love for her was

---

[1] Jeremiah's younger contemporary, Habakkuk (chap. 1), also raised similar issues. The question is, of course, later discussed with some length in the Book of Job.

first manifested in delivering her from the hand of the Egyptians, after which He entered into a covenant relationship with her: 'Ye have seen what I did unto the Egyptians, and how I bare you on eagles' wings and brought you unto myself. Now therefore, if ye will obey my voice ... and keep my covenant, then ye shall be a peculiar treasure unto me from among all peoples. .... And all the people answered together and said, All that Yahweh hath spoken we will do' (Ex. 19: 4–5, 8; cf. also Ex. 24: 3). Yet Israel had more than once broken her obligations to this covenant. Referring to Israel's election by Yahweh and to her subsequent unfaithfulness to Him Amos represents Yahweh as saying, 'You only have I known of all the families of the earth: therefore I will punish you for all your iniquities' (Amos 3: 2); while again Yahweh says through Hosea, 'They have broken my covenant and transgressed my law' (8: 1, R.S.V.). The terms of the ancient covenant seem to have been expressed anew in Josiah's law-book and are probably preserved in Deuteronomy 26: 17–18[1]: 'You have declared this day concerning the Lord that he is your God, and that you will walk in his ways, and keep his statutes and his commandments and his ordinances, and will obey his voice; and the Lord has declared this day concerning you that you are a people for his own possession, as he has promised you, and that you are to keep all his commandments, that he will set you above all nations that he has made ...' (R.S.V.). But not many years later Jeremiah complains of the failure of the Israelites to keep the ordinances laid upon them consequent to their delivery from the land of Egypt (7: 22–26). Yahweh now says of them: 'You shall call to them, but they will not answer you. And you shall say to them "This is the nation that did not obey the voice of the Lord their God, and did not accept discipline; truth has perished; it is cut off from their lips" ...' (7: 27–28, R.S.V.).

This infidelity of the Israelites to the covenant terms was as much a problem for the prophets as it was the cause of their denunciations. Thus, Hosea complained of the transgressions of the covenant (8: 1) but his firm belief in the unfailing love of God

---

[1] Wheeler Robinson, *Inspiration and Revelation in the Old Testament*, p. 154.

for his people also prompted him to represent Yahweh as saying:
'How can I give you up, O Ephraim! How can I hand you over,
O Israel! How can I make you like Admah! How can I treat you
like Zeboiim! My heart recoils within me, my compassion grows
warm and tender' (11 : 8, R.S.V.). Similarly, on his call Isaiah
conceives of Yahweh's anger being maintained against his people
'Until cities be waste without inhabitant and houses without men,
and the land become utterly waste' (6 : 11), but his hope that
Yahweh's anger might yet be averted also leads him to say,
'Turn to him from whom you have deeply revolted, O people
of Israel' (31 : 6). Hence, on the one hand these prophets believed
that a just God would exact retribution from His people, while
on the other they were convinced of His unfaltering love for
Israel.[1] Consequently they experienced the difficulty as to how
God's justice should be reconciled with His mercy and as to how
Israel should be brought to that degree of repentance which would
merit the exercise of God's love towards her.[2]

Jeremiah was the first of the prophets of Israel to deal effectively
with this problem. His predecessors had thought in terms of the
nation and consequently regarded sin from the national standpoint. Analysing the cause of sin Jeremiah traced it to the wickedness of the human heart (4 : 14): it was due to 'a stubborn and
rebellious heart' that the people sinned (5 : 23). Sin was not,
however, natural or necessarily innate in man. On the contrary it
was natural for man to adhere to the standards of his god even
though that god were an idol (2 : 11). So in obedience to nature
'the stork in the heavens' and other fowls of the air fulfil the law
of their being (8 : 7). Israel alone 'among the nations' of the world
says 'We will follow our own plans, and will every one act
according to the stubbornness of his evil heart' (R.S.V. 18 :
12–13). But man may become so depraved through wilful disobedience that sin binds him like iron cords: 'The sin of Judah is
written with a pen of iron; with a point of diamond it is engraved

---

[1] The concept of Yahweh's unceasing mercy towards His chosen people receives
greater emphasis in such passages as Hosea 11 : 9; and Isaiah 31 : 4–5, the genuineness of
which is, however, doubtful.
[2] Cf. N. H. Snaith, *The Distinctive Ideas of the Old Testament*, 1950, pp. 120–121.

on the tablet of their heart' (17: 1). During his early ministry the prophet had preached the need for repentance, maintaining that only in acknowledgement of guilt could restoration to Yahweh be effected (3: 12 f.; 4: 1–4). Moreover, man is not without the faculty of free-will. As the potter can remould a piece of clay which has assumed a faulty pattern (18: 3–4) so, by implication, the sinner can desist from his evil ways and resolve to lead a life in accordance with the will of God. But man's indifference to sin and his long association with it produces a state of moral bondage whereby he refuses even to consider the possibility of release from it: 'They do not say in their heart let us fear the Lord our God' (5: 24). At length Jeremiah became convinced that Israel could not of her own accord return to Yahweh: 'Can the Ethiopian change his skin or the leopard his spots? Then also you can do good who are accustomed to do evil' (13: 23). So strong is the influence of habit that sin has now become part of man's nature rendering him helpless in its toils. If, then, man is to be delivered from this bondage the initiative must spring from God; and this must take the form of the bestowal of grace rather than retributive punishment. No less than the earlier prophets Jeremiah believed in God's unfailing love for Israel: 'I have loved you with an everlasting love; therefore I have continued my faithfulness to you' (31: 3). But Yahweh will now manifest this love in a new way: 'Again I will build you, and you shall be built' (31: 4). Yahweh's earlier covenant relationship with the nation was effected by the sprinkling of blood upon the altar and upon the people as a whole (Exod. 24: 6–8), thus signifying the superficial nature of the bond which subsisted between God and man.[1] This covenant was in consequence subject to many limitations. It was primarily regarded as being contracted with a national deity rather than with a spiritual and universal God, while because of its external nature it failed to effect any radical change in the heart of man. Jeremiah had witnessed the end of the nation and recognised that the notion of a formal covenant contracted with a

---

[1] Cf. W. R. Smith, *The Religion of the Semites* (3rd edn., 1927), p. 318; J. Pedersen, *Israel*, I–II, p. 285.

national deity had now become unrealistic; but he was more perturbed by the falsity of conceiving of man's relationship to God in this way. A new and more adequate statement of this relationship must be attempted. He therefore conceives of God as saying: 'I will make a new covenant with the house of Israel and the house of Judah, not like the covenant which I made with their fathers when I took them by the hand to bring them out of the land of Egypt, my covenant which they broke . . . But this is the covenant which I will make with the house of Israel . . . says the Lord: I will put my law within them, and I will write it upon their hearts; and I will be their God, and they shall be my people. . . . I will forgive their iniquity, and I will remember their sin no more' (31: 31–34).[1] God's love for man is so steadfast that His mercy even extends to forgiving past sins and iniquities, while on the heart thus cleansed He will bestow His grace. Jeremiah had long been aware that sin sprang from the wickedness of the human heart but now that God will implant His law there the whole nature will be transformed. The inward and spiritual nature of this relationship will enable man to attain an immediate consciousness of God and consequently to direct fellowship with Him.

In thus making a changed heart a necessary condition of communion with God Jeremiah was again the first exponent of the principle that religion is a matter between God and the individual soul. Nor could any other conception of religion have been adequate to the exigencies of the time in which he lived. For only a spiritual and universal conception of God could have survived this age of social and cultural dissolution. Great empires had run their course and so had the state religions which depended on them. Confronted with the challenge of international movements and forces the heathen gods had been powerless to preserve the state and had failed the individual in his hour of need. Thus

[1] Duhm (*Das Buch Jeremia*, pp. 237 f.) questioned the Jeremianic authorship of this passage. For arguments substantiating its genuineness see Skinner, op. cit., pp. 320–334; J. A. Bewer, op. cit., 2, p. 25; cf. also W. Rudolph, op. cit., pp. 170–171. However it may be argued that the language reflects the influence of later editors, the thought is essentially Jeremianic (cf. also 32, 40).

deprived of the solace of religion the individual was abandoned to a lot which he could only regard with indifference and despair. Judah, too, had ceased to exist as an independent state and the flower of her people had gone into exile, where, separated from the national sanctuary at Jerusalem, the question as to how Yahweh should be worshipped was acutely raised. Jeremiah solved this question, not by recourse to the doctrine of national religion, but by the declaration of the spiritual and forgiving nature of God who in His universal dominion could be worshipped wherever the heart of man sought Him sincerely. Far from despairing of the future the individual Israelite was assured that the age of true religion was but dawning and that through the direct approach of a clean heart it was possible to establish a fellowship with God inexhaustible in its spiritual richness and content. Thus from the religious problems arising out of the age and conditions of the exile Jeremiah was able to propound a doctrine of God which was not only in advance of the Israelite thought of his own day but is fundamental to any spiritual conception of the nature and being of Deity.

IV

THE JEWS IN EXILE

THERE can be little doubt that the Chaldean invasion of Judah was effected with all the severity of Jeremiah's utterances. A Babylonian source states that in March 597 Nebuchadrezzar 'besieged Jerusalem and seized it .... He then captured its king and appointed a king of his own choice, having received heavy tribute from the city'[1]. The discovery of the Lachish Letters in 1935 further confirms the biblical account of the invasion and destruction of Judah by the Babylonians[2]. Excavations at the site of ancient Lachish prove that the town was assaulted about 597, while some of the actual documents discovered there relate to the final invasion of Judah a decade later. In Jeremiah chapter 34, verses 6–7 we read that 'Jeremiah the prophet spake ... unto Zedekiah king of Judah in Jerusalem, when the king of Babylon's army fought against Jerusalem, and against all the cities of Judah that were left, against Lachish and against Azekah; for these alone remained of the cities of Judah as fenced cities'. The substance of this narrative is remarkably confirmed by Letter IV of the Lachish documents in which Hoshiah[3], a Judean officer in the field during Nebuchadrezzar's second invasion, reported to his commanding officer at Lachish in the following terms: 'For the signals of Lachish we are watching according to all the signals which my lord gave, because we do not see (the signals of) Azekah'.[4]

---

[1] *Chronicles of Chaldean Kings (626-556 B.C.)* p. 33, by D. J. Wiseman.

[2] Cf. D. Winton Thomas, P.E.F.Q.S., 1950, pp. 1 ff.

[3] This name is common in the book of Jeremiah, e.g., 42: 1; 43: 2.

[4] Lines 10–13, as translated by J. W. Jack, op. cit., p. 169. See also Harry Torczyner (Tur. Sinai), *The Lachish Letters*, vol. 1, Lond., 1938, pp. 78–89, for Letter IV, Transliteration and Translation.

We are thus able to follow the course of the Babylonian armies as they prepared for their final assault on Jerusalem, already apparently invested for some two years (2 Kgs. 25: 1–3). It seems that their renewed attacks were directed from the west and south-west whence, however, from some vantage point[1] Hoshiah was able to observe their advance. All the Judean towns except Lachish and Azekah had ceased to resist the enemy, and even Azekah was now on the verge of collapse. Lachish was destroyed shortly afterwards, enabling the Babylonian forces to concentrate on the conquest of Jerusalem. From the details with which the Lachish Letters supplement our biblical records we are able to gain some view of the military precautions taken by the Judeans in their last desperate stand against invasion.[2] We can observe the sentinels from their outposts communicating with the Lachish commander, who in turn was in contact with the authorities in Jerusalem.[3] In the capital itself we witness the despair of the military leaders as they appealed to Egypt for help,[4] while we can understand the tension and terror which the inhabitants of the besieged and stricken city (2 Kgs. 25: 3; Lam. 4: 9–10) experienced as they learned of the steady advance of the enemy. At length the walls of the city were breached, and the king with members of his army fled by night from the doomed fortress only, however, to be captured near Jericho and taken to Babylon (2 Kgs. 25: 4–7). Significantly interpreting these events as the end of the national life of Judah, the Hebrew historian wrote: 'So Judah was taken into exile out of its land' (2 Kgs. 25: 21, R.S.V.).

In accordance with a practice commonly adopted by Assyrian rulers Nebuchadrezzar deported numbers of the Judeans to Babylon. Biblical and archaeological sources mention such captives. There is, however, some discrepancy in the biblical records of the numbers of exiles deported. Of the first deportation in 597, 2 Kgs.

---

[1] J. W. Jack thought that it was Mareshah, some 4 or 5 miles north-east of Lachish and 8 miles south of Azekah (op. cit., p. 185).

[2] Cf. A. Malamat, 'The Last Wars of the Kingdom of Judah', in J.N.E.S., 9, 1950, p. 225.

[3] Lachish, vol. I, Letter VI, lines 3–4; cf. also Letter XVIII.

[4] Lachish, vol. I, Letter III, lines 14–18; cf. Jer. 37: 6 f.; Ezek. 17: 15 f.

24: 14, 16 presents two different accounts. Thus in verse 14 we read that Nebuchadrezzar 'carried away ... all the princes, and all the mighty men of valour, even ten thousand captives, and all the craftsmen and the smiths'; while in verse 16 we find the record, 'all the men of might, even seven thousand, and the craftsmen and the smiths a thousand, all of them strong and apt for war, even them the king of Babylon brought captive to Babylon'. While, however, 2 Kings provides us with two records of the numbers deported in 597 it presents no record of the numbers deported in 586, apart from a reference to officials of the temple and to some 'threescore men' who were put 'to death at Riblah in the land of Hamath' (2 Kgs. 25: 18–21). It is unlikely that one of the records in 2 Kgs. 24: 14, 16 originally pertained to the account of the second deportation as narrated in 2 Kgs. 25: 8–22, as this account also appears in substantially the same form in Jeremiah 52: 9–27. An examination of the text of 2 Kgs. 24: 12–17 shows, however, the disarranged nature of the material contained therein. Verse 12 mentions the surrender of Jehoiachin and his household to Nebuchadrezzar, while verse 15 reports their deportation with the nobles of the land to Babylon. Verse 17 then states that Mattaniah was appointed vassal king of Judah by Nebuchadrezzar. This appears to have been the natural sequence of events in which the narrative is concerned with the deportation of the king and his court.[1] Syntactical considerations further suggest the displacement of verse 13. The phrase 'And he carried out thence' requires an immediate antecedent such as 'city', and hence seems to connect naturally with the end of verse 11 which reads, 'And Nebuchadrezzar ... came unto the city, while his servants were besieging it'. Apart from the mention of 'the princes' verse 14 seems to differ in substance from verse 16 only in its record of the deported. Of course it might be possible to argue that the figure 10,000 of verse 14 does not include 'the craftsmen and the smiths' mentioned later in the verse and who are specifically reported in verse 16 as amounting to 'a thousand'. Yet the appearance of the seven thousand 'men of might' in

---

[1] G. A. Montgomery, 'Kings', I.C.C., p. 556.

verse 16 suggests that it is a repetitive variant of the ten thousand 'men of valour' of verse 14, unless the terms גבורי־החיל and אנשי־החיל refer to different categories of people. The fact, however, that the records are given in terms of thousands indicates that the writer was dependent on tradition, and the appearance of two different figures suggests further that there were even variants of that tradition.[1] Moreover, it is doubtful if the sources from which Kings was originally compiled contained a record of the numbers of exiles, because such a source seems to have been used in Jeremiah 29: 2 where there is a reference to the deportation of Jehoiachin and his household as well as 'the princes of Judah and Jerusalem, and the craftsmen and the smiths' without, however, any mention of the numbers deported.

This discrepancy in the record in 2 Kgs. 24: 14–16 is accentuated by the fact that in Jeremiah 52: 28–30 we have another record of the numbers of Jews deported to Babylon. Although these verses are not represented in the Septuagint, the introductory sentence 'This is the people whom Nebuchadrezzar carried away captive' indicates that we have preserved here an extract from official records of the captivity. The text then reads: 'In the seventh year, three thousand Jews and three and twenty: in the eighteenth year of Nebuchadrezzar he carried away captive from Jerusalem eight hundred thirty and two persons: in the three and twentieth year of Nebuchadrezzar, Nebuzaradan the captain of the guard carried away captive of the Jews, seven hundred forty and five persons: all the persons were four thousand and six hundred'. Maintaining that a distinction is to be observed between the 'Jews' of verse 28 and the captives 'from Jerusalem' in verse 29, some scholars read the 'seventh' year of verse 28 as the 'seventeenth' year of Nebuchadrezzar, and have accordingly regarded the figures mentioned in these two verses as referring to one and the same deportation.[2] Nebuchadrezzar's 'seventeenth' year would then refer to his

---

[1] Cf. J. W. Wevers, 'Double Readings in Kings', J.B.L., 65, 1946, pp. 307–310. Some scholars accept the figure of 10,000 as being substantially accurate; cf., e.g., A. Malamat, op. cit., p. 223, n. 22; cf. also G. A. Cooke, 'Ezekiel', I.C.C., 1936, pp. xxxv–xxxvi.

[2] W. Rudolph, Jeremiah, H.A.T., p. 281; J. A. Bewer, *The Book of Jeremiah*, 2, p. 86; Volz, *Studien zum Text des Jeremias*, Leipzig, 1920, pp. 344–345.

subjugation of the Judean towns a year or two prior to his capture
of Jerusalem in 587-6. In view of the destruction of these towns
as mentioned in both the biblical and Lachish sources it is likely
that considerable numbers of Jewish peoples were taken captive.
It is unlikely, however, that the comparatively large number of
3,023 should be transported from the smaller towns, while only
832 should have been deported from Jerusalem which was completely subjugated. Further, this change of the 'seventh' to the
'seventeenth' year of Nebuchadrezzar entirely ignores the Babylonian attack on Jerusalem in 597 when according to the tradition
in 2 Kgs. some eight or ten thousand people were deported to
Babylon. The historicity of the deportation mentioned in
Jeremiah 52: 30 is also questioned.[1] Yet a transportation of the
Jews is reported by Josephus (*Ant.* X, 9, 7) in his account of
Nebuchadrezzar's subjugation of Egypt in the 'twenty-third'
year of his reign, in 582; and it is significant that Jeremiah on his
descent to Egypt after the fall of Jerusalem delivered an oracle
against Egypt predicting its destruction by Nebuchadrezzar
(Jer. 43: 8 f.). In order to dispose of the reference in Jeremiah
(52: 30) to a deportation of the Jews in 582 Volz resorts to considerable emendation of verses 29-30. Thus by transferring the
figure mentioned in verse 30 to the context of verse 29, and
then assuming that the entire reconstructed passage refers to the
Babylonian campaign of 588-586 he concludes that verse 29
should read: 'in the eighteenth year of Nebuchadrezzar, Nebu-
saradan ... carried away out of Jerusalem 832 persons, 745
Judeans'.[2] This combination of figures on the grounds that they
must refer to one deportation does not affect the estimate of the
total number of exiles, because Volz accepts the figure of 3,023
for the deportation of 597; but it is questionable if a rendering
obtained by such drastic emendation represents the original text.

While then the records of 2 Kgs. 24: 14, 16 appear to be disarranged and contain much that is secondary, the precise and

---

[1] Rudolph, ibid.; J. Begrich, *Die Chronologie der Könige von Israel und Juda*, Tub.,
1929, p. 201; Volz, ibid.

[2] Ibid.

5

modest figures of the records in Jeremiah 52 : 28–30 indicate that
they emanate from a source which is reliable in its information.[1]
The combined figures recorded here amount to only 4,600 people,
but this cannot be said to represent the total aggregate deported.
For in accordance with the Oriental custom of enumerating the
populace, by which men only were counted, women and children
were not included here.[2] The entire number of the Jewish people
deported to Babylon by Nebuchadrezzar cannot then have been
less than fourteen or fifteen thousand souls.[3]

But, although we cannot determine with accuracy the total
number of the Jews deported to Babylon, we are enabled, however, to follow their fortunes there with reasonable certainty.
C. C. Torrey of course could write: 'As for those inhabitants of
Jerusalem and Judea who were deported to Babylonia, we have
no good reason to suppose, but very good reason to doubt, that
any portion of them constituted a settlement that was ever heard
of again.'[4] Yet biblical references and archaeological evidence
indicate that the Jews in Babylonia maintained contact with the
remnant in Jerusalem and that they lived in settlements under
comfortable conditions. We know of one definite instance in
which Jeremiah sent a letter to the exiles through the agency of
Palestinian ambassadors to Babylon; and he doubtless took
advantage of other similar opportunities of corresponding with
them (cf. Jer. 29 : 31). Moreover, the false prophets who were in
Babylon were able to send 'letters' to 'all the priests' and to 'all

---

[1] Regarding the record in Jer. 52 : 28–30 as 'an extract from an official document of
the Babylonian golah giving exact figures for the three deportations' and commenting
on the disparity of this record with that of 2 Kgs. 24 : 14, 16, W. F. Albright says: 'The
difference may be partly due to the fact that the latter was only a conjectural estimate, but
may also be partly due to the heavy mortality of the starving and diseased captives during
the long trek to Babylonia' (*The Biblical Period*, 1950, p. 47).

[2] Cf. *The Jewish Encyclopaedia*, vol. 3, p. 564, Lond., 1902.

[3] R. H. Pfeiffer, accepting the basic figures of Jer. 52 : 28–30, calculates a total exiled
population of 18,000 (*Hist. of New Test. Times*, New York, 1949, p. 169). According to
Josephus, a total of 13,832 people were deported in 597 (*Ant.*, X, 6, 3; X, 7, 1). But he
seems to have reached this number through a confusion of the figures of 2 Kgs. and Jer.
52. Thus, he states that 3,000 (cf. Jer. 52 : 8) were deported immediately after the death of
Jehoiakim, while three months later 10,832 (cf. 2 Kgs. 24 : 14 and Jer. 52 : 29) were deported
with Jehoiachin. He gives no figures for the deportation of 586.

[4] *Pseudo-Ezekiel and the Original Prophecy*, New Haven, 1930, p. 33.

the people that were at Jerusalem' (Jer. 29: 26). It is likely that it was through these communications that Jeremiah learnt of certain developments amongst the exiles. Indeed it was largely through such correspondence that the hope was maintained that Jehoiachin would eventually return to Jerusalem, and which in the meantime led many to regard him as the rightful king of Judah. Such information as the book of Jeremiah affords us on this question is, however, supplemented by archaeological data.

Excavations conducted at ancient Debir and Beth-Shemesh during the years 1928–1930 yielded a find of three stamped jar handles each bearing the inscription לאליקים נער יוכן . The inscriptions on each of the three handles are perfectly legible and are so identical in every respect that it is probable that all three were stamped by the same seal. Professor Albright who was himself present when two of the seals were found has been the first to draw attention to the significance of these discoveries for the history of Israel during the exile.[1] The inscriptions may be rendered 'To Eliakim Steward of Joiachin' from which it may be inferred that Eliakim was acting in the capacity of administrator of the property of Jehoiachin. But it is doubtful if these seal impressions were struck during the reign of Jehoiachin who only occupied the throne during a period of three months when Jerusalem was besieged by the Babylonians (2 Kgs. 24: 8, 10). Normal business transactions for which the seals were used would hardly continue while the city was besieged. It is more likely that they were used after Jehoiachin's deportation to Babylon, when, with Zedekiah's enthronement as a vassal of Nebuchadrezzar, peace was restored to Judah. The reason for striking these seals in the name of Jehoiachin can only be understood on the assumption that the Jews remaining in Palestine still considered Jehoiachin as their legitimate king and only regarded Zedekiah as acting as regent. The discovery of yet two more seals belonging to the same period serves to establish the probability of this conclusion.[2] One,

[1] 'The Seal of Eliakim and the Latest Pre-Exilic History of Judah', J.B.L., 51, 1932, pp. 77–106.
[2] H. G. May, 'The Three Hebrew Seals and the Status of Exiled Jehoiachin', A.J.S.L., 56, 1939, pp. 146 ff.

discovered at the site of ancient Mizpah, reads, ליאזניהו עבד המלך—
'To Jaazaniah Servant of the King'. Epigraphical considerations
suggest that the name on this seal is to be identified with 'Jaazaniah' one of 'the captains of the forces' who 'came to Gedaliah to
Mispah' on the occasion of Gedaliah's appointment to the
governorship of Judah (2 Kgs. 25: 23).[1] Gedaliah, however, was
only 'Governor' while Jaazaniah is represented on the seal as
declaring his loyalty to 'the king'. But as H. G. May points out
Zedekiah and his sons were now dead and so the only person who
could be regarded as king would be Jehoiachin.[2] Moreover,
Judah was now a Babylonian province, and as this seal could
hardly be used without the knowledge of Babylon it is likely that
its use was permitted because even the Babylonians themselves
regarded Jehoiachin as king of Judah. In fact in certain cuneiform
texts discovered in Babylon and published recently by E. F.
Weidner[3] Jehoiachin is mentioned as 'King of the land of Judah'.
The other seal which concerns us here was found at the site of
ancient Lachish and bears the inscription לגדליה אשך על הבית
'To Gedaliah who is over the House'.[4] It is unlikely, in view of
the other seal, that this can refer to any other than 'Gedaliah
Governor' of Judah. The significance of the inscription lies in its
representation of him as על הבית—Over the House—a title which
in earlier Israelite history has been applied to a regent (cf. 2 Kgs.
15: 5; 2 Kgs. 10: 5).[5] So now it is probable that the person for
whom Gedaliah was acting was none other than Jehoiachin who
was in exile in Babylon.

No doubt the activity of the nationalist prophets in Jerusalem
did much to attribute this regnal status to Jehoiachin. For,
although Zedekiah had been reigning already four years (Jer.
28: 1) we hear utterances to the effect that 'within two years'

[1] W. F. Badè, 'The Seal of Jaazaniah', Z.A.W., 10, 1933, pp. 150–156.

[2] Op. cit., p. 147. It will be remembered that Zedekiah was an uncle of Jehoiachin
(2 Kgs. 24: 17) and also that his sons were slain by Nebuchadrezzar (2 Kgs. 25: 7).

[3] 'Jojachin-König von Juda in babylonischen Keilschriftexten' (*Mélanges Syriens
offerts à M. René Dussaud*, vol. 2, 1939, pp. 923–935).

[4] S. H. Hooke, P.E.F.Q.S., 1935, pp. 195 ff.

[5] For examples in which this term denotes 'regent', see H. G. May, op. cit., p. 147,
n. 7.

Yahweh would restore 'Jeconiah (Jehoiachin) the son of Jehoia-kim, king of Judah with all the captives of Judah' (Jer. 28:4; cf. also 27:6). From the passages in Jeremiah's letter advising the exiles to ignore the promises of their false prophets it may be assumed that similar hopes were circulated in Babylon (cf. also Jer. 29:24–32). Moreover, we know that Jehoiachin was main-tained in honourable circumstances in Babylon. The cuneiform tablets published by Weidner not only refer to him as 'King of the land of Judah', but mention that, together with his five sons, he received liberal allowances of oil and food. The circumstances of the discovery of the tablets would suggest that Jehoiachin lived in a house of some size; but in any case the fact that his sons are here reported as being 'in the hands of' an attendant not only proves that he was able to marry and rear a family, but also that he had his own servants.[1] His fellow exiles would be aware of these favourable circumstances of Jehoiachin, and would report accordingly to their brethren in Jerusalem. Such news would in turn inspire the hope amongst the Judeans that Jehoiachin would return and resume his sovereignty over them. This conception of his kingly status even in exile must have become the accepted Jewish view of a later generation, for the historian writing after 560 could still refer to Jehoiachin as 'king of Judah' (2 Kgs. 25:27). The editor of the book of Ezekiel also reckoned the chronology of Israel in terms of 'king Jehoiachin's captivity' (Ezek. 1:2).

After the restlessness of the first few years the Jews seem to have followed the advice of Jeremiah and settled down to life in the exile. Archaeological and biblical evidence testifies that they lived in settlements in various parts of Babylonia. During the years 1893 to 1896 the Babylonian Expedition of the University of Pennsylvania discovered a number of cuneiform tablets on the banks of the canal Kabari on which the ancient town of Nippur was situated.[2] The tablets prove to be the records of a Babylonian

---

[1] See W. F. Albright, 'King Joiachin in Exile', B.A., 5, 1942, pp. 49–55.
[2] H. V. Hilprecht and A. T. Clay, *Babylonian Expedition of the University of Pennsylvania*, Series A, vols. 9–10, 1898, 1904.

business house, Murashu Sons, which was established at Nippur
in the fifth century. Several of the tablets contain Israelite names
common to the books of Ezra and Nehemiah and thus indicate
the existence of a Jewish colony which settled here following
deportation by Nebuchadrezzar.[1] Ceramic evidence found within
a radius of some miles north and east of the site also suggests that
Jewish people continued to live in the vicinity until the final
destruction of the town in about A.D. 900. The historical significance of Nippur is likewise attested by Jewish tradition
inasmuch as the Talmud identified the Calneh of Genesis 10 : 10
with Nippur.[2]

The canal Nar Kabari on which Nippur was built is also
identified with the river Chebar[3] on the banks of which, in the
company of fellow exiles, Ezekiel experienced his first vision
(Ezek. 1 : 1). Close to the river Chebar there was another centre
of the captivity, Tel-abib, to which Ezekiel came (Ezek. 3 : 15)
after this vision. The Hebrew תל אביב may be equated with the
Babylonian Til-abub, meaning 'mound of the deluge',[4] by
which the Babylonians referred to the mounds formed by alluvial
deposits. Jewish bowls found nearby suggest that the Israelite
colony of the biblical Tel-abib was located in this vicinity.

There were other centres of the captivity besides the settlements on the banks and vicinity of the river Chebar. In the lists
of returned exiles of Nehemiah chapter 7 (cf. Ezra 2) we find
mention of such places as Tel-melah and Tel-harsa (Neh. 7: 61)
as districts from which the captives had come. The element 'tel'
would suggest that such places were situated near the canal
Chebar or somewhere along the Euphrates; while the Baby-

[1] H. V. Hilprecht, *Explorations in Bible Lands*, Edin., 1903, pp. 409–410; cf. also E.
Ebeling, *Aus dem Leben der Judischen Exulanten*, Berlin, 1914 (Wissenschaftliche Beilage
zum Jahresbericht des Humboldt-Gymnasium).

[2] Order Moed, *Tractate Yoma 9b–10a*; cf. also E. B., 1, p. 632 (Lond., 1899). Albright
suggests that the Hebrew word 'calneh' should be pointed so as to read 'kullánáh',
'all of them' (J.N.E.S., 3, 1944, pp. 254–255). This would not, however, affect the
historical importance the Jews attached to Nippur.

[3] H. V. Hilprecht, 'Explorations in Bible Lands', p. 412; cf. also W. F. Albright,
'The Seal of Eliakim', J.B.L., 51, 1932, p. 100.

[4] W. F. Albright, ibid.

lonian names Cherub and Immer (v. 61) respectively mean
'house of tilled ground' and 'sheep house'[1] and indicate that the
Jews who lived here followed agricultural and pastoral callings.
Ahava, apparently situated on a Babylonian canal of that name
(Ezra 8: 15, 21, 31), is also mentioned in connection with the
sojourn of the exiles; while Casiphia, with its governor Iddo, is
mentioned as another centre (Ezra 8: 17) somewhere in the same
vicinity. According to Josephus, one of the biggest settlements
was a city called Neerda, which was 'not only a very prosperous
one, but one that had a good and large territory around it, and
besides its other advantages, full of men also' (*Ant.* 18, 9, 1).[2]
This city was evidently built somewhere on the Euphrates, for,
referring to another settlement in close proximity to Neerda,
Josephus said: 'There was also the city of Nisibis situated on the
same sweep of the river' (ibid.; cf. also 18, 9, 9). It appears,
however, that such communities as were settled on or near the
river Euphrates constituted only a minor element of the total
population of the Jewish exiles. For the biblical records state that
Nebuchadrezzar deported all the members of the royal household,
together with all the men fit for military service, to Babylon. The
cuneiform texts published by Weidner not only confirm that
Jehoiachin and his family had their quarters in Babylon, but also
testify to the presence of other Jews there.

There are many reasons, indeed, why the city of Babylon
should have been the chief centre of the captivity. Nebuchadrezzar
had only recently become ruler of the Neo-Babylonian empire.
His father, Nabopolassar, was the founder of the dynasty but was
so preoccupied in establishing himself over his newly won
dominions that he had but little time to devote to the capital
itself. Such domestic concerns awaited the attention of his son,
who, however, decided that the new Babylon should surpass the
glories of the fallen Assyrian capital of Nineveh. He needed much
labour for the accomplishment of his projects, but could ill afford

[1] W. F. Albright, op. cit., p. 101.
[2] For the significance of Neerda in Jewish history, see *Jew. Ency.*, vol. 9, pp. 208 f.,
Lond., 1905.

to engage the services of his own subjects as they were needed to maintain his authority throughout the provinces of his vast empire. Now, Berossus, the Babylonian historian, informs us that Nebuchadrezzar 'arranged that when the captives came they should be placed as colonies in the most suitable places of Babylonia',[1] and continues 'then he adorned the temple Belus in a most magnificent manner' (ibid.). Evidently the captives who were brought to Babylon were such as could be profitably employed in the reconstruction and adornment of the city. This explains why our biblical records mention the deportation of the craftsmen and artisans to Babylon (2 Kgs. 24: 14, 16) and why Weidner's texts mention Jewish names alongside the craftsmen and skilled workmen from other states.[2] These workmen participated in the building and adornment of Babylon, which Herodotus (1, 178) tells us became in the reign of Nebuchadrezzar the most elegant city of its day, and that its beautiful gardens and graceful architecture surpassed anything ever attempted by the most ambitious of Assyrian rulers.[3] And it must have been a source of some satisfaction to the Jews that their craftsmen, experienced since the days of Solomon, performed no insignificant part in the reconstruction of this new and magnificent city.

But although it may with some certainty be concluded that the Jews contributed to such constructions in Babylon it cannot be inferred that they were subjected to harsh or unpleasant treatment. Of course the Babylonian authorities were compelled to exercise restraint over the more seditious members of the exiles. For immediately after the first deportation the spirit of revolt and discontent was fostered by the false prophets (Jer. 29: 8, 15: cf. also 28: 3; Ezek. 13: 1–7) who themselves took such an active part in the conspiracies that Nebuchadrezzar put two of them to death (Jer. 29: 21–22). There can be little doubt that if the exiles submitted to the government of their Babylonian rulers they

---

[1] *Apud Josephus Ant.* 10, 11, 1.   [2] A.N.E.T., p. 308 b.
[3] Cf. here G. Contenau, *Everyday Life in Babylon and Assyria* (the period 700–530 B.C.), Eng. trans., Lond., 1954, pp. 34–41.

would have been allowed to live in peace. Indeed, Jeremiah was aware of this, for, as we have already seen, in his letter to the exiles he advised them to disregard the messages of their prophets and to 'seek the welfare of the land' of Babylon, to marry and establish homes and to become loyal citizens of the state (Jer. 29: 7). The exiles might even attain to a position of prosperity; for houses, gardens, fruit, and domestic happiness was the prophet's conception of life in Babylon. Accordingly, there are indications that after the initial distaste of the 'golah' had passed the more enterprising of the exiles availed themselves of the opportunities which their new environment offered. Place names in Nehemiah chapter 7 indicate that many of them were settled on fertile mounds. Here they would have been able to raise crops and plant gardens which produced abundant fruit, and so prove the truth of Rabshakeh's description of Babylonia as 'a land of corn and wine, a land of bread and vineyards, a land of oil, olives, and honey' (2 Kgs. 18: 32).[1]

In addition to the more rural occupations there is also evidence that the Jews were engaged in the mercantile life of the great Babylonian capital. All the great highways converged at Babylon which now became the centre of the commerce of the Near East. It was a city built 'on many waters rich in treasures' (Jer. 51: 13) and had become 'the praise of the whole earth' (Jer. 51: 41). It is not surprising to find that the Jews who had a wide interest in commerce since the trading pursuits of Solomon (1 Kgs. 9: 26, 28; 10: 22, 29) should now become active in this 'land of traffic', this 'city of merchants' (Ezek. 17: 4). That they sought 'the welfare of the land' in the prosperity associated with its commercial activities may be demonstrated from certain archaeological material. Thus, a tablet containing a cuneiform inscription published by T. G. Pinches,[2] proves to be the record of a transaction between an Israelite and a Babylonian during the period of exile. The record relates to a dispute over profits between a

---

[1] Cf. G. Contenau, op. cit., pp. 41–43, for the fertility of Mesopotamian soil.

[2] *The Old Testament in the Light of Historical Records of Assyria and Babylonia*, Lond., 1908, p. 458.

certain Nabunaid and Aahau son of Saniawa, and Pinches pointed out that Saniawa is but one of the many names ending in 'iawa' which represents the characteristically Hebrew ending 'iah'. As Subunu-yawa represents the Hebrew Shebaniah (Neh. 9 : 4) so now Saniawa is but the Babylonian equivalent of the Hebrew Shaniah. But more significant still as a testimony to the commercial activities of the Jews in Babylonia is the evidence furnished by the Murashu business records already mentioned. On these records Jewish names are prominent amongst the clients of the vast banking and brokers establishment which transacted business at Nippur. Dating from 464 to 405 these records testify to the extent to which the Jews had established themselves in Babylonian business concerns by the early fifth century.[1]

A consideration of the language spoken in Babylonia during the exile will further assist us in studying the conditions under which the Jews lived there. It has long been recognised that the official language spoken in the time of the Persian empire was Aramaic;[2] but it is now known that Aramaic was also the language of the Neo-Babylonian empire. Indeed there is evidence that the Aramaic language had been used by the Assyrians since the days of Tiglath-Pileser III in the eighth century. For the advantages of the Aramaic script were such that it would be used by any progressive ruler. Early in their history the enterprising Arameans adopted the linear script from the Phoenicians.[3] In the course of their trading expeditions to Egypt they also became acquainted with the scribal device of pen and ink which they readily recognised as convenient accessories to the new alphabet.[4]

---

[1] A. T. Clay, *Business Documents of Murashu Sons of Nippur*, in University of Pennsylvania Publications of the Babylonian Section, vol. 2, no. 1, pp. 1–54, 1912; cf. also, G. Contenau, op. cit., p. 85. The census lists of Ezra 2 and Nehemiah 7 probably belong to the period of about 440 B.C. (cf. Albright, 'The Bible After Twenty Years of Archaeology (1932–1952)', in *Religion in Life*, 21, no. 4, 1952, p. 547). Although the wealth attributed to the returning exiles is stated with some exaggeration in these lists, they nevertheless reflect the degree of affluence to which the exiles attained in Babylon.

[2] Martin Noth, *Die Welt des Alten Testaments*, Berlin, 1953, p. 180. The Aramaic portions of Ezra represent correspondence with the Persian court.

[3] Cf. G. R. Driver, *Semitic Writing* (Schweich Lectures, 1944), chap. 3; R. A. Bowman, 'Arameans, Aramaic, and the Bible', J.N.E.S., 7, 1948, p. 73.

[4] J. H. Breasted, *Ancient Times* (2nd rev. edn.), 1935, p. 186.

The alphabetic script, as developed by the Arameans, and the Egyptian pen and ink combined then to produce a facile and effective system of writing. Through the travels of the Aramean merchants, and the Assyrian transportations of Aramean populations, the Aramaic language quickly spread to many parts of the Assyrian empire. As early as 729 summaries in Aramaic appear on the margin of cuneiform business records enabling the contents of the records to be comprehended at a glance.[1] But Aramaic was used in Assyria for other than commercial purposes. A seal impression in Aramaic, describing the status of an official of the household of Sargon, has been discovered at Khorsabad demonstrating that the language had been used in a literary capacity towards the end of the eighth century.[2] The royal Assyrian monuments, on which an Aramaic scribe with pen and parchment is depicted standing beside an Assyrian scribe, indicate that all booty taken in war was recorded in Aramaic as well as in Assyrian from the eighth century onwards.[3] The well-known incident of the visit of the Assyrian military mission to Jerusalem in the reign of Hezekiah testifies to the diplomatic use of Aramaic at this time (2 Kgs. 18: 17–27). In order to negotiate in secret with the Assyrians the Judean officers said to the Assyrians: 'Speak . . . in the Aramaic language, for we understand it', thus proving that by 700 Aramaic had been recognised as the medium of diplomatic exchange. It is not, however, only in Assyrian and Palestinian contexts that we read of the use of Aramaic, for archaeological evidence also points to the use of the language in official circles in Egypt by the middle of the seventh century.[4] Especially significant as a witness to the recognition of Aramaic by the Egyptian Pharaoh at the end of this century is the papyrus fragment discovered at Saqqara in Egypt in 1942. The fragment is written in Aramaic in a square script such as we find in our

[1] R. A. Bowman, op. cit., pp. 74–75; G. R. Driver, op. cit., pp. 121–123.
[2] M. Sprengling, 'An Aramaic Seal Impression from Khorsabad', A.J.S.L., 49, 1932, pp. 53–55.
[3] A. T. Olmstead, *History of Assyria*, Lond., 1932, pp. 178–179; cf. also J. H. Breasted, op. cit., pp. 187–188.
[4] R. A. Bowman, op. cit., p. 76.

Hebrew Bibles.[1] The document reflects the troubled conditions of Palestine round 603 and contains a request from Adon, king of Ashkelon,[2] to the Pharaoh for help against the threatened approach of the Babylonians.[3] It is thus not only an important historical record, but is a remarkable illustration of the employ-ment of Aramaic as an international court language. For while it is not surprising that the sender of the letter did not use his own language, which was probably some Canaanite dialect, he might, however, be expected to address the Pharaoh in Egyptian. His use of Aramaic can only be explained on the grounds that by his day Aramaic had been recognised as the diplomatic tongue of the Near East.[4]

It will at once be seen that this widespread use of the Aramaic language by 600 B.C. had a direct and significant bearing on the conditions of the Jews in Babylonia. Instead of having to learn Babylonian and adapt themselves to the use of its cumbersome script they found on their arrival in Babylon that the recognised tongue of the day was Aramaic, a language that differed from their native Hebrew only to the extent of mere dialectical peculiarities. We have seen that since the reign of Hezekiah the military officers could speak Aramaic, and as most of the Jews deported to Babylonia were of the higher classes of society they had but little difficulty in accommodating themselves to the linguistic requirements of their new environment. It will be recalled moreover that Arameans, distant kinsmen of the Hebrews, were among those deported tribes who contributed to the down-fall of the Assyrian empire,[5] and now, doubtless, formed a significant element of the population in Babylonia.

The Arameans, however, would not be the only kindred people whom the Jews would meet in Babylon, for it is also

---

[1] John Bright, 'A New Letter in Aramaic Written to a Pharaoh of Egypt', B.A., 12. 2. 1949, pp. 46–52.
[2] So H. L. Ginsberg, B.A.S.O.R., 3, 1948, pp. 24–27, and Bright, op. cit., pp. 48–49.
[3] Lines 6–7.
[4] John Bright, op. cit., p. 51.
[5] For the Assyrian deportation of Aramaic populations, see D. D. Luckenbill, A.R.A.B., 1, pp. 269–276.

probable that they came into contact with the descendants of the Israelites who were deported from Samaria over a century earlier. It was during that phase of Babylonian conquest that Babylonia had been annexed to Assyria,[1] and it is therefore likely that the Israelites from Samaria were transported to this province. Ezekiel certainly seems to have come into contact with the people of Israel and to have exercised a common ministry amongst the peoples of both Israel and Judah (cf. e.g., Ezek. 16: 15). His prophecies regarding the ultimate union of both houses assume a most concrete significance in the light of these presuppositions. Thus Rudolph Kittel argued with some conviction that Ezekiel not only visualised a rehabilitation of the Jews in Palestine, but that the Israelites who had been deported from Samaria would, even in exile, be united with the people of Judah and with them return to Jerusalem.[2] The prophet's well-known vision of the dry bones in chapter 37 is certainly suggestive of this interpretation. For the dead and dismembered bones can only refer to the divided and defunct kingdoms of Israel and Judah, while the simile of the revivification of these bones signifies the ultimate resurgence and reunion of both kingdoms: 'Son of man, these bones are the whole house of Israel . . . I will . . . cause you to come up out of your graves, O my people; and I will bring you unto the land of Israel' (vv. 11–12). The simile of the joined sticks in verses 15 f. continues this same theme: 'Behold I will take the stick of Joseph, which is the hand of Ephraim, and the tribes of Israel, and I will put them with it even the stick of Judah and make them one stick and they shall be one in mine hand' (v. 19).[3] Only an audience composed of

---

[1] Luckenbill, op. cit., 2, p. 818; A. T. Olmstead, *Hist. of Assyria*, pp. 255 f.

[2] *Geschichte des Volkes Israel*, 3, pp. 112 f. Indeed the evidence for Ezekiel's connection with the northern tribes is so strong that J. Smith argued that the prophet himself was deported with them in 734 and that certain passages of his book were delivered to these tribes then (*The Book of Ezekiel, a New Interpretation*, Lond., 1931, p. 91). Cf. here also G. A. Cooke, 'Ezekiel', I.C.C., p. 397.

[3] Verse 22 is more emphatic still in its portrayal of the union of the 'two nations' under one king, although perhaps bearing the signs of later editing: 'I will make them one nation in the land, upon the mountains of Israel; and one king shall be king to them all; and they shall be no more two nations, neither shall they be divided into two kingdoms any more.'

representatives of both the Israelite and Judean peoples could have provided the immediate background of these words of Ezekiel.

Perhaps it was in accordance with the practices already observed by the northern Israelites that Jewish life in the exile was organised mainly on a communal basis.[1] The elders resumed their ancient significance in the life of the community. Thus we hear of 'the elders of the house of Israel' (Ezek. 14: 1; 20, 1) and 'the elders of the house of Judah' (Ezek. 8: 1); and in accordance with the increased influence of their position Jeremiah's letter is addressed chiefly 'to the elders of the captivity' (Jer. 29: 2). Ezekiel who was concerned with the spiritual welfare of both houses presided over the gatherings of the elders in somewhat the same way as Samuel at an earlier date presided over the affairs of the tribes (1 Sam. 7: 5, 15; 8: 4; cf. also 2 Kgs. 6: 32). Such occasions provided Ezekiel with opportunities to deliver certain oracles and religious addresses. He was himself married (24: 18) and lived in his own house (8: 1): he moves freely from one place to another and nowhere is there an atmosphere of fear or oppression. The exiles were also free to meet him and to discuss religious matters, and the frequency with which such assemblies took place could only have been possible to a people enjoying both freedom of religious expression and the amenities of civic life. As W. O. E. Oesterley pointed out, the Israelites who had been residing in Babylonia since the time of Sargon would long since be regarded as nationals and would therefore be entitled to all the liberties and conveniences granted to citizens of the day.[2] And to some extent this is the position of the Judeans as they are represented in the Weidner tablets. Jehoiachin himself is married and has five sons:[3] he has his own attendants and is generously supplied with the necessaries of life. But the royal family is no exception in this respect, for other 'men from Judah' also appear on the tablets as

---

[1] Cf. here A. Causse, *Du Group Ethnique à la Communauté Religieuse*, Paris, 1937, pp. 187 f.

[2] Op. cit., 2, p. 47; cf. also Oesterley and Robinson, *Hebrew Religion*, 2nd edn., 1937, pp. 283–284.

[3] A.N.E.T., p. 308 (c); cf. also 1 Chron. 3: 17 f., which reports the names of seven sons of Jehoiachin.

receiving such bounties.[1] The conception of life in the exile which may be gathered from the book of Ezekiel together with the honourable treatment accorded the captives in the Weidner tablets combine, then, to justify the conclusion that the lot of the exiles in Babylonia was not one of persecution or degradation.

In the light of such considerations we may call in question the conclusions of some writers who have depicted the sojourn of the Jews in Babylonia as one of suffering and slavery. Thus, Ewald, from a few selected references in Isaiah, Lamentations, and the Psalms, concludes: 'We can no longer trace the historical details, but we are safe in drawing the general conclusion that the sufferings in the exile were . . . rendered continually greater and heavier until at last universal despair may well have seemed ready to overpower the whole race'.[2] Similarly, J. Meinhold could speak of 'the oppression of bondage' under which the Jews 'lived' and of 'the impassioned hatred against Babylon' which may be seen from the Jewish lyrics and oracles of the time.[3] We cannot, of course, overlook the feelings of depression and loneliness which certain biblical references reflect (e.g., Is. 42: 22; 47: 6; Ps. 137: 1 f.).[4] The humiliation with which the Jews conceived of the exile would in itself be bound to find some expression. A Babylon which had ruined the hopes of a Judean national resurgence, destroyed her cities and temple, and which, moreover, had deported the flower of her race could not be kindly remembered by the exiles. Deutero-Isaiah was then only expressing the wishes of his people when he said: 'Come down and sit in the dust, O Virgin daughter of Babylon . . . sit thou silent

---

[1] A.N.E.T., ibid. [2] *History of the Jews*, 5, p. 7 (Eng. trans.).
[3] *Einfüherung in das Alte Testament*, 2nd edn., Giessen, 1926, p. 240.
[4] Commenting on Is. 47: 6 and 50: 6, the Jewish scholar L. Finkelstein observed: 'The prophet is altogether unaware of the true conditions of his exiled countrymen in Babylonia' (*The Pharisees*, 2, Philadelphia, 3rd impress., 1946, p. 630); cf. also pp. 456–461. So with regard to similar references in Deutero-Isaiah R. H. Pfeiffer remarked: 'The poet's fancy pictures their condition in the darkest colours in order to enhance the brilliance of their coming triumph. . . . Moreover, if Israel is the servant suffering and dying for the salvation of mankind . . . its present misery and plight must needs be magnified beyond the bounds of actual fact.' (*Intro. to the Old Test.*, p. 464.) Again it is possible that such passages derive from a period subsequent to the exile when the Jews experienced certain disappointments.

and get thee into darkness, O daughter of the Chaldeans; for thou shalt no more be called 'The lady of the kingdoms' (Is. 47: 1–5). It was those exiles who had formerly cherished the continuance of the Josianic state and revelled in the splendour of the cleansed temple who were naturally most indignant towards the conqueror: well indeed might Babylon be reminded, 'Upon the aged thou hast very heavily laid thy hand' (Is. 47: 6).

But while there are such references to the sovereignty of Babylon and to the humiliations of the exiles these references do not in themselves justify the conclusion that the Jews in Babylonia suffered physical ill-treatment or that they experienced any civic disadvantages or religious persecutions. While there is no direct biblical evidence for any persecution under Nebuchadrezzar, there is, on the contrary, a reference to the leniency of Evil-Merodach in 'setting' Jehoiachin's 'throne above the thrones of the kings that were with him in Babylon', in inviting him to dine at his own table, and in granting him a liberal allowance of the good things of life (2 Kgs. 25: 27–30). We have no record of Neriglissar's disposition towards the Jews; but he came to power as a usurper and it is likely that during the four years of his reign he was so preoccupied in maintaining himself against conspiracy that he had but little opportunity of materially interfering with them. His son Labashi-Marduk was a minor when he ascended the throne, and it is unlikely that he pursued a policy of the persecution of the exiles during the nine months of his chaotic reign. From the zeal with which Nabonidus embraced the worship of the god Sin he can scarcely be quoted as being favourably disposed towards the religion of the Jews: nevertheless, the interest which he showed in the gods of Babylonia might also have been his attitude towards the Hebrew religion. Moreover, as we have earlier seen, from the fourth to the twelfth year of his reign he was absent in Arabia, from whence he withdrew only because he either suffered, or feared, defeat at the hands of Arabian and Persian troops. Arrangements for the defence of Babylon against the expected advance of the Persians must have engaged his attention on his return, and it is doubtful if in such a crisis he would have dissipated his energies in persecuting the Jews.[1]

It seems then that the evidence which may be derived from recent archaeological as well as from biblical sources regarding the conditions of the Jews in exile only combines to confirm the conclusion reached by Sir George Adam Smith over a quarter of a century ago when he said: 'There is every reason to believe . . . that this captivity was an honourable and easy one.'[2] But, as we have already argued, this is not to say that the Jews did not experience a sense of humiliation on being deported to Babylon, nor that they did not express their indignation against their captors. We have recognised moments of frustration and depression, of sadness over the desolation of Jerusalem, and of longing for the worship enjoyed in the precincts of the temple. Yet not even from the most pessimistic interpretation of the evidence for the conditions of the Jews in exile could we conclude that their experiences were anything approaching the severities endured by the Jews in Europe in the Middle Ages when they were subjected to the humiliation of wearing a yellow badge to distinguish them from the Christians, and of being compulsorily secluded in the narrow confines of the Ghetto.[3] But even while living under such degrading conditions these Jews were able to make invaluable contributions to the development of Christian philosophy in Europe. A significant feature of this contribution is 'the fact that it was largely due to Jewish writing that Aristotelian teaching could be accommodated to biblical doctrine'.[4] It is not therefore surprising that under infinitely more favourable circumstances the exilic prophets produced the most creative thought of all Hebrew literature.

[1] In an article, 'Nabonidus and the Later Jewish Exiles', J.T.S., April 1951, pp. 34–44, J. M. Wilkie maintained that the Jews suffered religious persecution under Nabonidus. It is questionable, however, if the evidence justifies his conclusion, 'The Jewish exiles in this period were being subjected to religious persecution' (p. 42).

[2] *Book of Isaiah XL–LXVI*, new edn., 1927, p. 59; cf. also O. C. Whitehouse, *Expositor*, May 1923, pp. 321 f.; Rudolph Kittel, *The Religion of the People of Israel* (Eng. trans.), Lond., 1925, pp. 160–161; Reuben Levy, *Deutero-Isaiah*, Oxford, 1925, p. 7; Martin Noth, *Geschichte Israels*, Gött., 1950, p. 256.

[3] Cf. R. T. Herford, in *The Legacy of Israel*, Oxford, 1948 edn., pp. 97–128.

[4] C. and D. Singer, 'The Jewish Factor in Medieval Thought', in *The Legacy of Israel*, p. 252.

6

V

EZEKIEL AND THE EXILES

THE circumstances of Ezekiel's ministry represent a new stage in the history of Yahweh's revelation of Himself to His people. For Ezekiel was the first of the great prophets to be commissioned to work in a land outside Palestine. The chief tenets of his teaching were propounded in answer to the pressing religious and moral problems which confronted the early exilic community, and herein lies the significance of his work.

The Book of Ezekiel is, however, one about which there is less agreement amongst modern scholars than any book in the Old Testament. The confidence with which writers at the beginning of the century accepted its Ezekelian authorship and Babylonian setting in the time of the exile[1] has given place to present-day uncertainty and confusion on these same questions. The publication in 1924 of Hölscher's *Hesekiel, der Dichter und das Buch*, in which he accepted little more than a seventh of the book as genuine, may be said to represent the beginning of this scepticism. C. C. Torrey's *Pseudo-Ezekiel* published in 1930 was more startling still; for Torrey not only denied Ezekelian authorship and the Babylonian background to the prophecies, but argued that the book is a third-century Palestinian redaction of an earlier pseudograph purporting to be written in the reign of Manasseh. In the following year another publication appeared connecting the book with the reign of Manasseh: this was, *The Book of Ezekiel, a New Interpretation*, by J. Smith. Unlike Torrey, how-

---

[1] Cf., e.g., G. B. Gray, *A Critical Intro. to the Old Test.*, 1913, p. 198; S. R. Driver, *Intro. to the Lit. of the Old Test.*, 9th edn., p. 279; H. A. Redpath, *The Book of the Prophet Ezekiel*, 1907, p. xiv; E. Kautzsch, 'Religion of Israel', H.D.B., 5, pp. 701 f. (1906); cf. also Davidson and Streane, *The Book of the Prophet Ezekiel*, Camb. Bible, pp. xxi f. (1916).

ever, Smith accepted the historical ministry of Ezekiel, claiming that he was one of the northern Israelites deported by the Assyrians in 734 but that he returned again to Palestine in 691, 'the thirtieth year' (Ezek. 1: 1) after the fall of Samaria. Henceforth the prophet preached against the idolatry so rampant in Jerusalem under Manasseh's reign. The Palestinian background for the book thus advocated was further emphasised by Herntrich who, in his *Ezechielprobleme* published in 1932, argued that Ezekiel never went to Babylon at all but exercised his entire ministry in Jerusalem in the reign of Zedekiah. He regarded the term 'house of Israel' as referring to the Jews of Judah and Jerusalem where the prophet was himself living 'in the midst of a rebellious house' (12: 2), while the Babylonian setting and chapters 40–48 are to be attributed to the pen of a later writer.

Henceforth scholars were prepared to consider the possibility of this view. Thus in 1934 Oesterley and Robinson, discussing the question of a twofold ministry, remarked that 'Whether Herntrich's conclusions be accepted or not it must be allowed that they go a long way in solving the problem of the book',[1] and further expressed the opinion that Ezekiel began his ministry in Jerusalem in about 602 but in 597 he was carried captive to Babylon where he continued to minister to his fellow exiles.[2] Two years later A. Bertholet published his commentary 'Hesekiel' (H.A.T., 1936) in which he suggested that Ezekiel prophesied in Jerusalem from 593 till the final fall of the city: he was then taken captive with the second deportation and began another ministry amongst the exiles. Although attributing the Babylonian background and other parts of the book to the hand of a redactor Bertholet ascribed a certain nucleus of chapters 40–48 to Ezekiel. R. H. Pfeiffer also advocates a double sphere for the prophet's ministry. According to him Ezekiel was carried to Babylon in 597 with the first captivity. In 593, while amongst the captives at the river Chebar, he received a call to prophesy to the people of Jerusalem: obeying

---

[1] *Intro. to the Books of the Old Test.*, p. 325.

[2] Op. cit., p. 328. So in the second (1953) edition of *Prophecy and the Prophets in Ancient Israel*, T. H. Robinson wrote: 'There is . . . a tendency to think of Ezekiel as a prophet who worked in Jerusalem, perhaps only in Jerusalem' (p. 146).

the call he immediately journeyed to the city where he worked till it was besieged by the Babylonians in 587. Escaping from the doomed city, the prophet managed to return to Babylonia where he worked amongst the exiles till about 571.[1] Another American scholar, W. A. Irwin (*The Problem of Ezekiel*, 1943), also postulates a double ministry for the prophet's activities. Ezekiel, he claims, prophesied in Jerusalem till the fall of the city in 586, after which he was taken to Babylon where he uttered some prophecies of hope to the exiles. Irwin, however, confines the genuine prophecies of Ezekiel to about a quarter of the present book, the rest being the product of a later editor. In a work which appeared posthumously Wheeler Robinson expressed himself in favour of the view taken by Bertholet and accordingly thought that 'the historic Ezekiel prophesied in both Judea and Babylon';[2] while Aage Bentzen inclined rather to the view of Pfeiffer when he was prepared to consider the possibility that Ezekiel received his call in Babylon in 593 and then returned to Jerusalem in the capacity of a prophet.[3] Rejecting the exilic date for Ezekiel, Nils Messel in his *Ezechielfragen* (1945) argued that the prophet spent his entire ministry in Palestine as late as 400 B.C. Somewhat similar to this view is the position of L. E. Browne who in a publication entitled *Ezekiel and Alexander* recently (1953) propounded the thesis that Ezekiel was a contemporary of Alexander the Great and was himself responsible for the exilic setting of the book.

It will be observed that a number of scholars within the past three decades have postulated a double scene for Ezekiel's ministry, and according to W. A. Irwin 'this is now the dominant view'.[4] But the traditional view has also had its champions within recent years. It was the position adopted by G. A. Cooke in 'The Book of Ezekiel' (I.C.C.) which appeared in 1936. While admitting that 'everywhere throughout the book, successive editors have been at work, collecting stray oracles, adding comments of their own, emending what seemed to be at fault'

[1] *Intro. to the Old Test.*, 1948, pp. 535–544.
[2] *Two Hebrew Prophets* (ed. E. A. Payne), Lond., 1948, p. 75.
[3] *Intro. to the Old Test.*, vol. 2, 1952, p. 127–128.   [4] *V.T.*, vol. 3, 1, 1953, p. 61.

(p. xxvi), Cooke regarded Ezekiel as a prophet of the Babylonian exile who uttered or wrote most of the material of the book that bears his name. The researches of C. G. Howie were especially concerned to defend and to rehabilitate the traditional view of Ezekiel, and in 1950 he published his book, *The Date and Composition of Ezekiel*,[1] in which he states as his conclusion that 'the traditional view of Ezekiel is substantially correct throughout' (p. 102). In an article entitled 'Aspects of the Book of Ezekiel' published in 1952, C. J. Mullo Weir similarly defended the Babylonian background and exilic date of the prophet's ministry.[2] More recently still H. H. Rowley in his article 'The Book of Ezekiel in Modern Study'[3] has supported the traditional claims for the book of Ezekiel. Arguing in favour of the unity and essential authenticity of the whole book, he concludes by placing the ministry of Ezekiel 'in Babylonia in the period immediately before and after the fall of Jerusalem' (p. 190).

Sufficient reference has been made to a representative selection of the writings and claims of modern scholars for us to realise that there is little unanimity in the present-day study of the book of Ezekiel.[4] The periods assigned to the prophet's ministry vary from the eighth to the fourth century. His activity has been placed exclusively in Babylonia or in Palestine, while a number of scholars argue for the exercise of a ministry in both places. Views on the authenticity of the book range from those who regard almost the entire material as Ezekielian to those who ascribe to the prophet scarcely an eighth of the book which bears his name.

Yet there seems to be some indication that the problem of the book is reducing itself to certain limits. The extreme views of

[1] J.B.L., Monograph Series, vol. LV, Pennsylvania.
[2] V.T., vol. 2, 2, 1952, pp. 97–112.
[3] B.J.R.L., vol. 36, 1, Sept. 1953, pp. 146–190.
[4] For fuller surveys of the views of the many scholars who have been engaged on a study of Ezekiel, see S. Spiegel, H.T.R., 24, 1931, pp. 245–321; W. O. E. Oesterley, *Church Quarterly Review*, 106, July 1933, pp. 187–200; C. Kuhl, T.R., N.F., 5, 1933, pp. 92 ff., 20, 1952, pp. 1 ff.; R. H. Pfeiffer, *Intro. to the Old Test.*, 1948, pp. 525–531; O. Eissfeldt, in *The Old Test. and Modern Study* (ed. Rowley), 1951, pp. 153–158; W. A. Irwin, 'Ezekiel Research since 1943', V.T., Jan. 1953, pp. 54–66; H. H. Rowley, 'The Book of Ezekiel in Modern Study', B.J.R.L., Sept. 1953, 36, 1, pp. 146–190.

Torrey and J. Smith have found little following, while those who posit a post-exilic date for the life and activity of the prophet fail to recognise fully the historical implications of the book. By confirming many biblical references and offering much independent evidence archaeological discoveries have demonstrated the historical reality of the exile. That the references in the book of Ezekiel to the river Chebar (1 : 3 ; 3 : 15, 23 ; 10 : 15, 20, 22) 'in the land of the Chaldeans' (1 : 3) bespeak historical facts is testified by the discovery of the Murashu documents at ancient Nippur. As we have seen, these documents presuppose the existence of well established Jewish colonies near this river before the fifth century, while the Weidner tablets actually mention Jewish exiles in Babylon itself. Jeremiah tells us that there were false prophets in the exile and there is no reason why a genuine prophet of Yahweh, such as Ezekiel, should not have been there. Moreover, only an exilic audience could account for the allusions in the book to Babylonian mythology and religion[1] as such allusions would have had no meaning for a Palestinian community. Thus, the elaborate descriptions of 'the four living creatures' seem to be drawn from the current Babylonian conception of certain astral deities.[2] The origin of the seven men who are represented as slaying the idolators in Jerusalem in Ezekiel's vision in chapter 9 is also probably to be found in the seven planetary gods of the Babylonian pantheon.[3] In chapter 21 : 21 we read that the king of Babylon decides to come to Jerusalem as a result of divination: 'He shook the arrows to and fro, he consulted the teraphim, he looked in the liver.' But while divination by arrows and the teraphim was known among the Western Semites, hepatoscopy, divination by the examination of the livers

---

[1] Cf. L. Dürr, *Ezechiels Vision von der Erscheinung Gottes*, Würzburg, 1917; C. H. Toy, 'The Babylonian Element in Ezekiel', J.B.L., vol. 1, 1881, p. 63; also J. Meinhold, *Einführung in das Alte Test.*, 1926, pp. 242–244.

[2] Oesterley and Robinson identify the 'creatures' with Nebo, Nergal, Marduk, and Ninib (*Hebrew Religion*, 1914, p. 274). Cf. also G. R. Driver, 'Ezekiel's Inaugural Vision', V.T., 1, 1, 1951, pp. 60–63, for the view that the imagery of Ezekiel's vision was suggested to him by 'the work of a Babylonian brass founder' (p. 62). Elsewhere Driver remarks on 'the number of Babylonian terms . . . and the Babylonian custom of judges "standing" in court, which Ezekiel seems to know' (*Biblica*, 35, 1954, p. 312).

[3] Oesterley and Robinson, ibid.

of animals, was a specialised function of certain members of the Babylonian priesthood; and as a reference to such divination occurs nowhere else in the Old Testament it is likely that it is this Babylonian practice of divination which is referred to here.[1] Such adaptations of Babylonian mythology and religion to the circumstances of his own day not only imply that the prophet was resident in Babylon but presuppose familiarity with Babylonian culture on the part of his audience. And however it may be argued on the grounds of literary criticism that the references to Tel-abib, the river Chebar and the captivity are insertions of the Babylonian Redactor, the prophet's use of Babylonian concepts which naturally lend themselves to his purpose cannot be discounted on the same grounds.

Moreover, apart from the references to 'Jehoiachin's captivity' by which the years are now reckoned (1 : 2; cf. also 19 : 8)[2] there are a number of historical allusions in the book which are particularly relevant to the events of the Near Eastern world during the years 609 to 573.[3] Thus in 19 : 3–4 where we read of one of the 'whelps' which was brought 'with hooks unto the land of Egypt' there is an obvious reference to Jehoahaz who was carried to Egypt after the death of Josiah in 609 (2 Kgs. 23 : 29 f.), while the other 'whelp' of the following verses 'who was brought to the king of Babylon' (19 : 9) probably refers to Jehoiachin who was deported to Babylon in 597.[4] In 17 : 13 f. there is a clear reference to Zedekiah's accession as a vassal of Nebuchadrezzar and also to his subsequent conspiracy with Hophra of Egypt in 587. Chapter 12 : 10–13 further refers to the capture of Zedekiah, to his blinding and eventual exile in Babylon, while chapter 33 : 21 mentions the fall of Jerusalem 'in the twelfth year' of the 'captivity'. The oracles against foreign nations (chs. 25–32) also point to the years immediately following the fall of Jerusalem.

---

[1] Cf. G. A. Cooke, op. cit., pp. 232–233; see also P. Haupt, 'Babylonian Influence in the Levitical Ritual', J.B.L., 19, 1900, pp. 56–61, 80.

[2] W. F. Albright, J.B.L., 51, 1932, pp. 93 ff.; also in B.A., 5, 1942, pp. 53–54.

[3] R. H. Pfeiffer, *Intro. to the Old Test.*, 1948, p. 532.

[4] Pfeiffer, ibid.; Cooke, op. cit., pp. 204–205; Wheeler Robinson, *Two Hebrew Prophets*, pp. 68–69.

Ammon, Moab (2 Kgs. 24: 2) and Edom (Jer. 27: 3) made pre-
datory incursions into Judah when Nebuchadrezzar first invaded
the land. On the eventual fall of the capital and the deportation
of many of the Judeans they would naturally be tempted to
increase and intensify their raids and plunderings. The oracle
against Tyre is dated 'in the eleventh year' which, if reckoned in
terms of Jehoiachin's captivity in 597, must be the year 586–5.
Independent historical evidence relates to Nebuchadrezzar's
designs on Tyre at this time. Josephus, on the authority of
Philostratus and Berossus[1] and on 'the reports of the Phoenicians',[2]
states that 'Nebuchadrezzar besieged Tyre for thirteen years'
(ibid.). The text which immediately follows is somewhat con-
fusing, but a reconstruction offered by Eissfeldt[3] indicates that
Nebuchadrezzar besieged Tyre in the seventh year of Ittobal III
(c. 586) and continued the siege for thirteen years when Ittobal
acknowledged the sovereignty of Babylon.[4] The city was
apparently not captured, but the discovery of contract tablets
dating from about 570 shows that henceforth it was governed by
Babylonian officials.[5] That Ezekiel was aware of this long and
unprofitable siege of Tyre may be seen from the contents of an
oracle against Egypt in 570 in which he says that although
Nebuchadrezzar subdued Tyre 'yet he had no wages . . . for the
service that he had rendered against it' (29: 18), but he will now
be rewarded in his efforts against Egypt in that 'he will take
her spoil and take her prey' (29: 19).

Neither are the oracles against Egypt which appear in Ezekiel
chapters 29–32 unconnected with historical events. Five of these
oracles are dated from the 'tenth' to the 'twelfth' year[6] and therefore apply to the years 587–585 when Egypt under the ambitious
Pharaoh Hophra was manifesting certain interests in Palestine. A

---

[1] *Against Apion*, I, 20.   [2] *Against Apion*, I, 21.

[3] 'Das Datum der Belagerung von Tyrus durch Nebuchadrezzar', F.u.F., 10, 1934,
pp. 164 f.; cf. also S. Spiegel, H.T.R., 24, 1931, pp. 291 f.; C. G. Howie, op. cit., pp.
42–43.

[4] C.A.H., 3, p. 302; cf. also F. K. Kienitz, *Die politische Gesch. Ägypt.*, p. 29.

[5] S. Spiegel, loc. cit.; G. A. Cooke, op. cit., p. xxxvii.

[6] 29: I is dated 'in the tenth' year; 30: 20 and 31: I 'in the eleventh'; and 32: I and
32: 7 'in the twelfth year'.

prophetic reference to a Babylonian conquest of Egypt is also preserved in Jeremiah 43 : 10–13, and pertains to the years following the fall of Jerusalem; and, as we noted in our last chapter, Josephus reports that Nebuchadrezzar made a punitive expedition against Egypt in 'the twenty-third' year of his reign, that is in 582 (*Ant.* 10, 9, 7). We have no extant Babylonian reference to a Chaldean expedition against Egypt before 568,[1] but even if this were the first time Nebuchadrezzar invaded Egyptian territory Ezekiel, who was living in Babylon, would have been aware of his intentions for some time. Certainly his latest and most threatening oracle against Egypt (29: 18–19) which may be placed at about 570[2] would have been delivered under these circumstances. The references to the Persians too as mercenaries of Tyre (27: 10) suggest that they were still an obscure and unorganised people, and must therefore refer to a period before 560 when they were unified into a powerful nation by Cyrus.[3]

These considerations then show that the oracular references in the book of Ezekiel to the nations of the ancient Near East are particularly relevant to the events of the period 609 to 570. The references, moreover, are of such a nature that they could only have been made by one who was himself a contemporary of the historical scene; and this consideration precludes the possibility that they derive from a later redactional hand.

It will have been observed that many scholars who accept the exilic date for Ezekiel's activity regard his ministry, however, as having been spent either wholly in Palestine or in Palestine as well as in Babylonia. Some maintain that the prophet worked in Jerusalem till the fall of the city in 586 and that he was then deported to Babylon where he continued his work amongst the exiles: others, again, hold that he received his call in Babylonia in 593 when he left immediately for Jerusalem, where he prophesied till the city was besieged and then escaped to Babylonia to continue his

[1] R. H. Pfeiffer, op. cit., p. 533; cf. also A.N.E.T., p. 308 (c).
[2] Cf. J. Finegan, 'The Chronology of Ezekiel, J.B.L., 69, 1950, p. 65.
[3] A. T. Olmstead, *The History of the Persian Empire*, p. 34.

ministry there. Yet the evidence which can be gathered from the book itself indicates that Ezekiel both received his call in Babylonia and that his entire ministry was confined to the exiles. The words in chapter 3 : 4 'Go, get thee unto the house of Israel and speak with my words unto them' are interpreted by some as meaning that the prophet visited Jerusalem in person on this occasion,[1] while the visions of Jerusalem described in chapters 8–11 are also thought to indicate the presence of the prophet in the city itself.[2] The fact, moreover, that most of the oracles in chapters 1–24 are directed chiefly against the Judeans led some scholars to postulate a Palestinian background for all this period of the prophet's activity.[3] The words 'Go, get thee unto the house of Israel' do not, however, demand for their interpretation that Ezekiel had to travel to Jerusalem to deliver his oracles there, and need imply no more than the words 'Go, prophesy unto my people Israel' as addressed to Amos (7: 15).[4] Nor must it be thought that the Jews of Jerusalem were regarded at this time as the true representatives of the 'house of Israel' and were therefore alone to be called by that name. On the contrary they were more than once declared by both Jeremiah and Ezekiel as the disobedient and doomed members of the race. No special notion of sanctity attached to the term 'house of Israel' and the evidence shows that it has been applied indiscriminately to the Jews in Judah and to those in the exile.[5] Of course, some movement on the part of Ezekiel to the scene of his first utterance is implied by the topography of our text. For while he received his call in some undefined place on the banks of the river Chebar (1 : 1–2) he afterwards 'came to them of the captivity at Tel-abib' (3 : 15) where there was a populous settlement. Moreover, the terms of his commission imply that he was being sent to his fellow Israelites

[1] E.g., R. H. Pfeiffer, op. cit., pp. 535 f.

[2] R. H. Pfeiffer, op. cit., pp. 536 f.; cf. also A. Bentzen, op. cit., 2, pp. 127–128; F. Horst, 'Exilsgemeinde und Jerusalem in Ez. viii–xi', V.T., 3, 4, 1953, pp. 337–360.

[3] E.g., Oesterley and Robinson, *Intro. to the Books of the Old Test.*, p. 319; Herntrich, *Ezechielprobleme*, pp. 82 f., 134 f.; Wheeler Robinson, *Two Hebrew Prophets*, p. 77.

[4] Cf. H. H. Rowley, B.J.R.L., Sept. 1953, pp. 173–177.

[5] J. Battersby-Harford, *Studies in the Book of Ezekiel*, Camb., 1935, pp. 31, 37, 93–101; C. J. Mullo Weir, op. cit., pp. 100–101; G. A. Danell, *Studies in the Name Israel in the Old Testament*, Uppsala, 1946, pp. 244 f.

who were living in the midst of 'a foreign people': 'for you are not sent to a people of foreign speech and a hard language, but to the house of Israel—not to many people of foreign speech and a hard language, whose words you cannot understand' (Ezek. 3: 5–6, R.S.V.). There would be no point in this reference to a foreign people unless the Israelites themselves were living in strange surroundings.[1]

Further, in the prophecy against Ammon we read 'Son of man, set thy face toward the children of Ammon, and prophesy against them' (25: 2); yet we are not to assume that Ezekiel uttered this in person in the land of Ammon: rather, the form of the oracle suggests that the prophet was speaking from a distance. The formulas, 'Son of man, set thy face toward the mountains of Israel, and prophesy unto them' (6:2), and, 'Son of man, set thy face toward Jerusalem... and prophesy against the land of Israel' (21: 2), may then be interpreted in the same way. The Babylonian setting of the texts relating to Ezekiel's call and commission is further confirmed by the symbolism employed in his first oracle concerning the fate of Jerusalem.[2] Not only was the tablet referred to as לבנה in chapter 4: 1 a Babylonian sun-dried brick, but the practice of drawing maps on such bricks was well known in Babylonia whereas we do not know of such a custom amongst the Jews of Judah.[3] Moreover, there would be little point in the symbolic representation of the city to the people of Jerusalem, nor would they need to be told 'This is Jerusalem' as in chapter 5: 5. Such representation would on the other hand impress on the exiles the reality of the forthcoming destruction of the city.

The directness with which the charges of idolatry and sin are made against the inhabitants of Jerusalem in chapters 8–11 is one of the reasons why some scholars place this phase of the prophet's ministry in Palestine.[4] But Ezekiel himself declares that the idolatry mentioned here is that represented to him by God in a

---

[1] Cf. C. J. Mullo Weir, op. cit., p. 101.

[2] For the character of Ezekiel's symbolism, see Georg Fohrer, *Die symbolischen Handlungen der Propheten*, Zürich, 1953, pp. 35–47.   [3] C. G. Howie, op. cit., p. 18.

[4] E.g., Oesterley and Robinson, Pfeiffer and Herntrich.

vision.[1] It was the vision which he experienced in 'the sixth
year' (8:1) and was similar to those he experienced earlier by the
river Chebar (1: 1–3; 3: 22). Thus he says: 'The spirit lifted me
up . . . and brought me in the visions of God to Jerusalem . . .'
(8: 3). In the visionary account that follows he is led round the
temple by God who bids him 'Go in, and see the wicked abominations that they do here' (8: 9). So prominent is the activity of God
in these chapters that it is only in a vision that Ezekiel could be
conceived of as witnessing it. The content of such a vision would
therefore have been as clear to him in Babylonia as in Jerusalem.
His familiarity with the temple before his captivity would enable
him to remember and to reproduce with accuracy the topo-
graphical details of the vision, while his characterisation of the
destroying angels in chapter 9 could have been suggested to him
by his knowledge of Babylonian mythology. That this was a
vision which Ezekiel experienced while living in Babylonia may
further be seen from his statement in chapter 11: 23 f. that the
'Glory of Yahweh went up from the midst of the city. . . . And
the spirit' brought him 'to them of the captivity' where he 'spake
unto them . . . all the things that Yahweh had showed' him.

It was appropriate that Ezekiel should at this time remind the
exiles of the idolatrous worship which was being practised in
Jerusalem and inform them of what Yahweh had said concerning
the people of Judah: 'Therefore will I . . . deal in fury: mine eye
shall not spare, neither will I have pity: and though they cry in
mine ears with a loud voice, yet will I not hear them' (8: 18).
For the exiles were now hoping to return to Jerusalem which
they regarded as being the only place where they could experience
the favour and blessing of Yahweh. Shortly before this Jeremiah
had written to the exiles advising them to ignore the utterances
of their false prophets, and implied the futility of hoping for an
immediate return to Palestine. Ezekiel now, dwelling 'in the midst
of' a 'rebellious house' (12: 2), had to contend with these same
issues. The false prophets still prophesied 'concerning Jerusalem
and' saw 'visions of peace for her' when there was 'no peace'

---

[1] Cf. here Harold Knight, *The Hebrew Prophetic Consciousness*, pp. 57–60.

(13 : 16) and still 'seduced' the 'people saying, "Peace", when there' was 'no peace' (13 : 10). In such circumstances it was necessary that Ezekiel should denounce the religious practices in Jerusalem and predict the imminent fall of the city and the consequent deportation of her king and her people (17: 19–21). Like Jeremiah, Ezekiel regarded the exiles as the only Israelites who would be called upon to bear God's message to a wider world. It is therefore not surprising that we should hear him, while in the presence of the exiles, utter oracles against Jerusalem in the hope that he would persuade them of the doomed state of the city and dissuade them from indulging in their vain hopes of returning there. And this further explains why in the genuine oracles against Judah there is no mention of a call to repentance, although the prophet himself was earlier reminded by Yahweh of this pastoral responsibility (3 : 18). For not only would the Judeans at a distance be insensible of such admonitions, but Ezekiel was convinced that the fate of Judah was decided and irrevocable.[1]

There are, of course, certain passages throughout chapters 1–24 which are suggestive of the view that Ezekiel entertained some ultimate hope for even the inhabitants of Judah and Jerusalem (cf. e.g., 6: 8; 11: 16–20; 12: 16; 16: 60–63; 20: 34, 40–42). If, however, any logical scheme is to be attributed to the mind of the prophet or to his teaching, such elements must be regarded as being the interpolations of later hands. Recognition of Ezekiel as an historical figure who lived and worked in Babylonia during the exile does not necessarily imply that he wrote or uttered all the material in the book which bears his name. For in common with the process of the compilation of all the prophetical books, the collection of Ezekiel's oracles continued for some time after his death and would therefore present an opportunity for extraneous material to be embodied in his work. Some critics, however, like Hölscher, Herntrich, and Irwin, have denied the whole of chapters 40–48 to the prophet. Yet Ezekiel was so concerned with the ultimate restoration of the Israelite people

---

[1] Cf. B. D. Eerdmans, *The Religion of Israel*, Leiden, 1947, pp. 197–198.

(chs. 34–37), and the exiles themselves so bewailed the loss of
the temple in Jerusalem that it is difficult to conceive of any
scheme of Israelite restoration without some reference to a temple.
The language which describes the visions in the earlier chapters of
the book bears a close affinity to that which is used in the descriptions of the visions of restoration in chapters 40–44, while a
prophet who was so grieved over the desecration of the temple in
chapters 8–11 would be likely to envisage a new building con-
secrated afresh to the service of God. Moreover, the conception
of an ideal sanctuary is more likely to have arisen during the
exile when the Solomonic temple lay in ruins than at any time
after the return, as the Second Temple completed in 516, however
modest a structure, would have been regarded as sufficient for the
needs of Jewish worship.[1] It is, therefore, likely that some nucleus
of these chapters must have derived from the prophet himself.
How much, however, as in the case of the earlier chapters of the
book, must remain doubtful.[2] But despite the uncertainty that
may prevail regarding the genuineness of certain passages and
chapters relating to the circumstances of the restored Israelites, the
authentic material throughout the rest of the book enables us to
study the work and teaching of the prophet. Indeed it might be
claimed that the passages through which Ezekiel transmits his
permanent and spiritual message to mankind are not seriously
affected by the critical analysis of the book.[3]

There is no good reason, then, to doubt the traditional view
that Ezekiel was transported to Babylon with the first deportation
of the Judeans in 597. He had been living there a few years before
his call to the prophetic office. The circumstances of his call in
Babylon were, however, as significant as those which charac-

---

[1] G. A. Cooke, op. cit., p. xxvi.

[2] Cf. here W. A. Irwin who said: 'As soon as one pushes beyond the general admission
of spurious matter in the book, and seeks to identify it, he is at once plunged into confusion and chaos.... Every scholar goes his own way, and according to his private
predilection chooses what is genuine and what is secondary.' (V.T., 1953, 3, 1, p. 61.)

[3] Speaking of the composite character of the book, W. A. L. Elmslie, however, said:
'While certain of its oracular passages are of pre-exilic date, these do not add any develop-
ment of thought not covered' by the 'great personalities' of the Old Testament. (*How
Came Our Faith*, Camb., 1948, p. 191, n. 1.)

terised the call of any of his great predecessors in Palestine. It will
be remembered that the accession of Psammetichus II (c. 594) to
the Pharaoh's throne was hailed by the Phoenician and Transjordan states as the signal for revolt against Babylon. Hoping to
enlist the support of Judah they sent their representatives to confer
with Zedekiah (Jer. 27: 3). We do not know how far the king
committed himself officially to the implications of this scheme,
but the occasion was interpreted by a nationalist prophet in
Jerusalem as grounds for predicting the early return of Jehoiachin
and his fellow exiles. The propagation of these rumours seriously
affected the Jews in Babylon where excitement ran so high that
Nebuchadrezzar put two of their leaders to death (Jer. 29: 22).

It was at this critical juncture in the history of the exiles that
Ezekiel received his call. We can therefore understand the urgency
with which he was told 'Go, get thee unto the house of Israel' to
'a rebellious house . . . to them of the captivity' (3: 4–11). These
circumstances of his call further explain the nature and order of
his addresses which follow. He hears from Yahweh the terms of
his commission: he is appointed a watchman to the exiles, and is
entrusted with a great responsibility. As a true pastor he must
warn his people of the danger of persisting in their sins and
iniquities: if he fails in his duties he himself will be held responsible for their lapses (3: 18). Rebellious Judah was the subject of
his first denunciations but he expects the exiles to be warned by,
and profit from, such utterances. The more arrogant of the
Judeans had hoped to defy Babylon, and had spread rumours of
the immediate return of their brethren from exile. Hence Ezekiel
immediately set about to dispel such hopes. Through symbolic
action he demonstrates the reality of the siege of Jerusalem
(ch. 4) and declares that Judah will resist Babylon only to be
destroyed by famine and sword (5: 16). There can be no mistake
as to the identity of this besieged city, for 'thus saith Yahweh. . . .
This is Jerusalem' (5: 5). Her sins and her wickedness even
exceeded the immorality of the surrounding nations who will
shortly witness her destruction and rejoice over her humiliation
and ignominy. Rebellious Judah is consequently a recurring

theme. For the city of Jerusalem had not yet fallen; and the prophet in a vision, experienced in 591, dramatically describes the idolatry which he sees practised in the temple (chs. 8–11). This flagrant adoption of heathen cults is, however, but an indication that Yahweh will not withhold his fury much longer (9:10).

Although Ezekiel was now speaking of the fate of the Judeans, the destruction of Jerusalem which he foretold was not under the circumstances welcome news to the exiles. For their prophets had led them to expect not merely a triumphant return to Palestine but to a Jerusalem preserved in all its former glory. Ezekiel's predictions were therefore not favourably received, and indeed he had been warned by Yahweh of such opposition when he was called to his mission (3:25). Hence he is again reminded by Yahweh that he is 'in the midst of' a 'rebellious house' (12:2) which is neither prepared to see the signs of approaching doom nor to hearken to his words, and he is accordingly instructed to repeat symbolically the details of the fall of Jerusalem and the attempt of Zedekiah to escape (12:3–12). Influenced by the prophetic predictions of hope the exiles, in common with the people of Jerusalem, believed that they were members of a privileged race which were entitled to the continuous protection of God. Yahweh would surely not allow his temple or his city to fall, but rather would preserve them as his people's rightful inheritance.

Ezekiel was thus compelled to point out the conditional nature of the inheritance of the Israelite people and the fatuity of the belief that they were of a distinguished and noble ancestry. In an oracle directed primarily against Jerusalem (ch. 16) he makes the startling, but historically true, statement: 'Your origin and your birth are of the land of the Canaanites; your father was an Amorite, and your mother a Hittite' (v. 3, R.S.V.). Making use of an old legend[1] he goes on to mention that Israel was but a foundling whom Yahweh rescued from obscurity, and by His grace and favour elevated her to a place of consequence and 'renown ... among the nations' (v. 14). But, alas, Israel showed

[1] See here G. A. Cooke, op. cit., pp. 159 f.

herself unworthy of this favour and, by yielding to the temptations of the heathen nations around her, was in fact but reverting to the conditions and standards from which she originally sprang. In this delineation of Israel's past Ezekiel is more penetrating and original in his condemnation of the nation than any of his predecessors.[1] Hosea attributed a measure of innocence to the nation when 'in the days of her youth' (Hos. 2: 15) she was called by Yahweh from Egypt, and he could represent Yahweh as saying, 'When Israel was a child, then I loved him' (11: 1). Jeremiah could also say that Yahweh remembered Israel for 'the devotion' of her 'youth' (2: 2, R.S.V.) while Isaiah could speak of 'the faithful city' and of her 'that was full of justice' (1: 21). These prophets recognised and condemned the sins which Israel committed, but whereas they were prepared to regard the Egyptian period of her history as one in which she behaved innocently and righteously Ezekiel could say, 'Thou calledst to remembrance the lewdness of thy youth' (23: 21). Ezekiel, too, knows of Israel's sojourn in Egypt and of her election by Yahweh there (20: 5, 9). But even then Israel was concerned with the idols of Egypt (20: 8), and much of her present iniquities can be traced to those days (23: 1, 8); for 'remembering the days of her youth, wherein she played the harlot in the land of Egypt' (23: 19) she now 'multiplied' her transgressions in similar directions. But, having chosen her, Yahweh for His 'name's sake' brought her 'forth out of the land of Egypt' (20: 9–10). 'In the wilderness' again 'the house of Israel rebelled against' Yahweh (20: 13). In the land of Canaan they also defiled themselves with idols (20: 28 f.), and later still fell a prey to the enticements of both Assyria and Babylonia (23: 12–17). So depraved had the Hebrews now become that the Philistines, inheritors of an advanced Aegean culture, were 'ashamed' of their 'lewd way' (16: 27).

By declaring Israel's racial connection with the idolatrous Semitic peoples, and in his thoroughgoing condemnation of every phase of her history, Ezekiel of course included the exiles.

[1] Cf. R. H. Pfeiffer, op. cit., p. 545.

7

But although the whole Israelite race is condemned, Judah, because of the special privileges accorded her, is even more guilty than Israel (16: 51; 23 : 11). Indeed comparisons may be extended beyond Samaria; for a Hittite mother and an Amorite father necessarily implies relationship with Sodom, her 'younger sister' (16: 46). Israel therefore has no racial superiority over the mixed peoples of Canaan,[1] and, because of her common relationship with these peoples, she herself can have no claim to any inherent virtue or godliness. An infringement of the conditions of her election by Yahweh in Egypt (20: 7) was not in itself sufficient to account for the present state of Israel's depravity. Ezekiel seems to know of a few righteous men (cf. 21 : 4) but the cause of Israel's sin is to be traced to the characteristics of her physical nature, to her ancestral connection with the Canaanite peoples who were by nature predisposed to a gross and sensual type of worship. In terms of later theology her people were possessed of 'Original Sin' which 'is the fault and corruption of the nature of every man'.[2] Any virtue therefore which the Israelites possessed was due to Yahweh's initial calling of them, to the fact already declared by one of their prophets that Yahweh had known them only 'of all the families of the earth' (Amos 3 : 2). Yahweh gave them the 'statutes of life' (33: 15; 20: 11) but now complains: 'The children rebelled against me; they walked not in my statutes, neither kept my judgments ... which if a man do, he shall live in them' (20: 21). The Israelites must have no illusions as to the consequences of their sins nor think that in adopting the moral and religious standards of the nations they may still communicate freely with God: 'Thus says the Lord God: Will you defile yourselves after the manner of your fathers . . .? When you offer your gifts and sacrifice your sons by fire, you defile yourselves with all your idols to this day. And shall I be inquired of by you, O house of Israel? As I live, says the Lord God, I will not be inquired of by you' (20: 30–31, R.S.V.).

---

[1] See G. A. Cooke, op. cit., pp. 160 f., for a discussion of the identity of the peoples designated Amorite and Hittite; also W. A. L. Elmslie, *How Came Our Faith*, pp. 98–99.

[2] Article 9 (of The Thirty-Nine Articles of the Church of England).

This alienation from God need not, however, be permanent because God in His mercy can restore the penitent and purified amongst them: 'I will bring you into the wilderness of the peoples, and there I will enter into judgment with you face to face. As I entered into judgment with your fathers in the wilderness of the land of Egypt, so I will enter into judgment with you, says the Lord God. I will make you pass under the rod . . . I will purge out the rebels from among you and those who transgress against me . . .' (20: 35–38, R.S.V.). The captivity is here represented under the figure of the wilderness to remind the exiles of Israel's former sojourn in a foreign land and of the travail of soul which she then experienced. Here, however, we notice that God will plead with them 'face to face' denoting that He will have intimate communion with them on matters of spiritual and personal moment.[1] In the homeland of Judah it was believed that Yahweh was only concerned with the nation and the community, but in Babylon the exiles would come to know that Yahweh was a God who could be approached individually and with whom personal communion could be made.

Accordingly Ezekiel was determined to teach the exiles a new value of the individual and, consequently, a new conception of God. The Israelite nation was in effect destroyed (17: 11–21). The whole land was impure; the royal house, priest, prophet, and people had all alike incurred unpardonable guilt (22: 23–31). It was therefore too late for intercession and repentance. The old Israel had come to an end, and the new era of the individual was about to be inaugurated.

But the exiles could not easily disregard the earlier tenets of their faith. Ezekiel condemned their past religious record; yet so persistent is the force of tradition that they were naturally influenced by the past in their concepts of Yahweh and religion. They had thought of religion and worship in terms of the nation and the temple, and the recently published Deuteronomic law emphasised these beliefs. Even the Judeans, who still had their altar and, to some extent, their nation, were saying 'Yahweh has

---

[1] Cf. Ex. 33: 11; Dt. 5: 4; Jud. 6: 22.

forsaken the land' (8: 12). Much more, then, had the exiles, separated from the temple and the nation, reason to contemplate the future with scepticism; and it is not surprising that we hear some of them say: 'Our transgressions and our sins are upon us, and we pine away in them; how then should we live?' (33: 10).

They were prepared to account for the present situation by citing the old proverb which they had known in Palestine: 'The fathers have eaten sour grapes, and the children's teeth are set on edge' (Ezek. 18: 2; Jer. 31: 29). In accordance with their communal conception of suffering they believed that the sons suffered for the sins of the fathers; and such was their notion of Yahweh that from the earliest times they believed that He visited 'the iniquity of the fathers upon the children to the third and the fourth generation'.[1] There is, of course, a sense in which any system of moral philosophy may vindicate the assumptions of this belief. But the Israelites now adhered to it to a degree which was destructive of all moral effort. For in addition to their general maxim the effects of the recent sins of Manasseh were thought to be inescapable (2 Kgs. 21: 11; Jer. 15: 4): such heinous crimes committed some fifty years earlier would have incurred a guilt which must prove ineffaceable for at least two or three generations. This doctrine of Yahweh's indiscriminate punishment for the sins of the past now raised disturbing questions for the exiles, and we hear them say, 'The way of Yahweh is not just' (18: 25). Some of Ezekiel's older prophetic contemporaries had experienced some misgivings on the question of the justice of God, but in the exile the problem had assumed new and dangerous proportions and therefore called for urgent attention.

The solution which Ezekiel offers to this pressing problem arises out of his conception of the being and nature of God. Unlike his contemporaries in exile he conceived of Yahweh as a God who was infinitely more than the national God of Israel. The exiles thought that because they were in exile they were abandoned by Yahweh to an indifferent fate; but Ezekiel was

---

[1] Ex. 20: 5; Num. 14: 18; Dt. 5: 9. See here J. M. Powis Smith, 'The Rise of Individualism Among the Hebrews', *Amer. Jour. of Theol.*, 10, 1906, pp. 251 f.

concerned to demonstrate that Yahweh's influence extended to all known lands and peoples. And particularly illustrative of this concept of the prophet are his oracles against foreign nations. Ammon had witnessed with satisfaction the destruction of Jerusalem and had rejoiced to think that her humiliation was complete. But the Ammonites had nursed a grievance against Israel since before the time of the Judges (Jud. 11: 4 f.), while their defeat and conquest by David (2 Sam. 8: 12 f.) aggravated this grievance. The passing years did little to improve relationships between the two peoples and when Nebuchadrezzar invaded the west the Ammonites willingly joined his forces in an attack against Judah (2 Kgs. 24: 2). Their duplicity became evident, however, when on a later occasion they tried to induce Zedekiah to join an alliance of the western states in a rebellion against Babylon (Jer. 27: 2 f.). On the fall of Jerusalem they again became hostile to the Judeans (Jer. 40: 14; 41: 10–15) and subsequently occupied Judean territory in Transjordan (Jer. 49: 2). It was therefore with exultant tones that they now scorned the fallen sanctuary at Jerusalem and derided those who were forced into exile (Ezek. 25: 2–6). But while Yahweh's temple may be destroyed and His people discomfited, His sovereignty over world events was not thereby affected. On the contrary He can say to Ammon: 'I have stretched out my hand against you, and will hand you over as spoil to the nations; and I will cut you off from the peoples and will make you perish out of the countries; I will destroy you. Then you will know that I am Yahweh' (25: 7).

Moab, too, was gratified with the fall of Judah. Her past relationship with Israel (cf., e.g., Num. 2–6; 2 Sam. 8: 2) suggested that the God Yahweh was more powerful than her own god Chemosh and consequently she assumed that Yahweh would protect His own land and people. It was then with some surprise, but with none the less satisfaction that she now remarked 'Judah is like all the other nations' (25: 8). There was no doubt some truth in this and the Moabites were but observing that Judah was no exception to the cosmic phenomenon of the rise and fall of nations. They must not, however, conclude that because Judah as a state had come to an end her God Yahweh was unable to protect her, being Himself defeated by the development of external political issues. Yahweh was independent of the continuance of any state and in His self-existence could say of Moab: 'I will give it along with the Ammonites to the people of the East . . . that it may be remembered no more among the nations, and I will execute judgments upon Moab. Then they will know that I am Yahweh' (25 : 10–11). Edom which 'cherished perpetual enmity' (35 : 5) against the Israelites and now 'grievously offended in taking vengeance upon them' (25 : 12) will likewise have cause to regret her actions. She was in fact a kindred people to Israel (Num. 20 : 14; Dt. 2 : 4; Amos 1 : 11) but this apparently only served to increase her envy. The fall of Jerusalem now incited her to further vindictiveness and we hear her say of the Judeans 'They are laid desolate, they are given us to devour' (35 : 12). But in the purpose of God the fall of Jerusalem was but one factor in a series of correlated events which would ultimately lead to Edom's destruction: 'Thus says the Lord God . . . As you rejoiced over the inheritance of the house of Israel, because it was desolate, so I will deal with you; you shall be desolate' (35 : 15). It was with evident pleasure that the Philistines also beheld the plight of Jerusalem. Since their defeat by David (2 Sam. 5 : 22–25) some four centuries earlier they had hostile dispositions towards the Hebrews and now thought that their hour of vengeance had come. But Yahweh will again compel them into submission and they will perforce recognise His power and acknowledge Him as Lord (25 : 15–17).

Ezekiel next turns his attention to Tyre. This city had been the subject of prophetic denunciation before (Jer. 25 : 22; 47 : 4; Joel 3 : 4), but Ezekiel indicts it with a severity unparalleled elsewhere in the Old Testament. This was doubtless due to the interest which the exiles were now manifesting in Tyre. Nebuchadrezzar was about to attack it and they consequently wondered if a people who had been equally rebellious as themselves against Babylon would suffer the same fate.[1] Shortly after the accession

[1] Cf. G. A. Cooke, op. cit., p. 287.

of Zedekiah Tyre had attempted to incite Judah to revolt against Babylon (Jer. 27: 2–4). But now that Jerusalem had fallen Tyre was only too ready to gloat over its destruction and to welcome the advantages which would in consequence accrue to herself, saying: 'Aha, the gate of the peoples is broken, it has swung open to me; I shall be replenished, now that she is laid waste' (26: 2). From an early date Tyre had been mistress of the sea (cf. 1 Kgs. 9: 27; 10: 11, 22) and had monopolised the maritime commerce of the ancient world. She would now, however, develop her inland trade with greater facility; for, the toll gates of Jerusalem being 'broken', her caravans would have free access to the trade routes of the Orient. But Tyre will not long enjoy the fruits of this project. For Yahweh will manifest His power over the 'riches', the 'merchandise' and the 'pleasant houses' of 'the renowned city' (26: 12–17): she 'that' dwells 'at the entrance of the sea . . . the merchant of the peoples unto many isles' and 'said, I am perfect in beauty' (27: 3) shall become 'a desolate city like the cities that are not inhabited' (26: 19). Tyre had drawn her wealth and resources from many countries: she obtained her timber from Lebanon, Bashan and Cyprus, her embroidery from Egypt and the 'isles of Elishah' (27: 5–7); sailors from Sidon, Arvad, and Gebal manned her ships (27: 8–9); the men of Lydia and Put contributed to her fighting forces (27: 10) while Judah, Damascus, Arabia and other countries bought her wares and enriched her treasuries (27: 17 f.). Yet although her influence and her power were so extensive that she could 'enrich the kings of the earth with the multitude' of her 'riches' and her 'merchandise' she shall 'be brought to silence in the midst of the sea . . . and will never be any more' (27: 32–36).

Tyre, however, is not the only great nation whose designs will be frustrated by Yahweh. Egypt will also experience the bitterness of a fallen power. Apart from the bondage in Egypt, Israel's association with that country was unfortunate and was always discountenanced by the prophets. Isaiah condemned Israel for taking 'refuge in the protection of Pharaoh' and for seeking 'shelter in the shadow of Egypt' (Is. 30: 2). Hosea regarded

Israel's overtures to Egypt as 'silly and without sense' (Hos. 7 : 11)
while Jeremiah was indignant at Judah's irresponsible schemings
with Assyria and Egypt (Jer. 2 : 36–37). Josiah's death at the hands
of Necho, and Judah's consequent subjection to Egypt cul-
minated in the arrival of Nebuchadrezzar in Jerusalem in 597 and
the submission of the city to his hands. A few years later when
Zedekiah was enthroned as a vassal of Babylon, Judah's reliance
on Egyptian help not only proved unavailing (Jer. 37 : 6; Ezek.
17 : 15) but had the effect of intensifying the Babylonian onslaught which eventually led to the destruction of Jerusalem.
Yahweh will now wreak vengeance on Egypt for this long and
tragic influence over Israel. Egypt 'shall never again be the
reliance of the house of Israel' (29 : 16). Her idols and images will
moreover be destroyed (30 : 13). Indeed on the question of
idolatry and religion Egypt was more reprehensible than Tyre.
For while Tyre boasted of her wealth and of the influence she
exerted over the nations of the Near East, the Pharaoh of Egypt
had arrogantly said, 'My river is mine own, and I have made it
for myself' (29 : 3). The Nile, which according to Herodotus
was 'a river differing in its nature from all other rivers',[1] had been
for centuries the source of life to the Egyptians.[2] It had irrigated
their fields and carried their water traffic, and the achievements of
the Egyptians could be seen in the many ways in which they
applied the forces of the Nile to their own welfare and advancement. Indeed the waters of the Nile had been responsible for the
advanced civilisation which was early developed in the Nile
Valley and which the Egyptians had now enjoyed for many
centuries.[3] But, however the Egyptians adapted the resources of
this river to their own needs and advancement, its life-giving
waters were ultimately the gift of God. In accordance with his
conception of himself as a divine being, the Pharaoh claimed that
the Nile was of his own fashioning, thus falsely arrogating for
himself a claim that could be made by Yahweh only. For this
vain and presumptuous boast the Pharaoh will be humbled: 'I

[1] Bk. 2, 35.   [2] Cf. Dt. 11 : 10.
[3] Cf. W. J. Perry, *The Growth of Civilisation*, Lond., 1937, pp. 44–51.

will bring a sword upon thee . . . and the land of Egypt will be
a desolation and a waste; and they shall know that I am the
Lord' (29: 8–9).

Such denunciations against Tyre and Egypt became more
assuring for the exiles when the prophet intimated that Babylon,
the great power which now wielded authority over them, would
also be involved in the scourge of the nations. For Babylon held
the sword by which these nations would fall: 'Thus saith the
Lord God: Behold I will bring upon Tyre Nebuchadrezzar king
of Babylon' (26: 7); 'he shall slay thy people with the sword,
and the pillars of thy strength shall go down to the ground'
(26: 11). In like manner, Nebuchadrezzar who had performed
'a great service against Tyre' would proceed against Egypt and
would humiliate her as the messenger and avenger of Yahweh
(29: 19–20). Ezekiel did not utter an oracle against Babylon
itself; for not only was the actual fall of Babylon in the distant
future, but an oracle of such a nature would only incur the host-
ility of Babylon against himself and the exiles. For the moment
it was sufficient that Babylon, the greatest power of the day,
should act as the avenging agent of Yahweh.

With the exception of Babylon, then, all the nations of the Near
East will be destroyed in order that they may acknowledge the
power and person of Yahweh. But this would not have as its
purpose a mere exhibition of Yahweh's power: it was rather
because, in the words of the Book of Genesis, 'the earth' had
become 'filled with violence' (6: 13) and because 'the imagina-
tion of man's heart is evil' (8: 21). Tyre especially deserved
destruction, because, through a false and elated pride, she said,
'I am a god, I sit in the seat of the gods', therefore Yahweh who
alone was 'God and not man' (Hos. 11: 9) rebuked her with the
words, 'You are but a man, and no god, though you consider
yourself as wise as a god' (Ezek. 28: 2, R.S.V.). Similarly,
because he was 'exalted in stature' and because he claimed that
the Nile was his own creation the Pharaoh of Egypt will be
humbled and 'driven out for his wickedness' (31: 10–11). Not
only was the majesty and sovereignty of God belittled by the

conceit of Tyre and Egypt but His holiness, which should be widely acknowledged, was violated by the pagan and degrading customs of the nations. It might be thought that in such contexts Ezekiel represents God as an egoistic being whose sense of His own existence is the justification of compelling men to 'know' Him. Yet the prophet's lofty conception of Yahweh serves partly to explain this representation of Him. He could fully subscribe to the conception of God held by the Deuteronomist: 'For Yahweh your God, he is God of gods, Lord of lords, the great God, the mighty, and the terrible, which regardeth not persons, nor taketh rewards' (Dt. 10: 17). It was, moreover, an age of international unrest and consequently of conflicting claims of many gods. Milcom of Ammon, Chemosh of Moab, Melkart of Tyre and the numerous gods of Egypt were doubtless regarded by their worshippers as superior to the God of Israel (cf. e.g., Ezek. ch. 25). To this rivalry were added the insults and injuries which many of these nations now inflicted upon the fallen Jerusalem (ibid.). Thus, in his indignation against such peoples, Ezekiel represents Yahweh as dealing harshly with them and regards their discomfiture justifiable if it leads them to acknowledge the incomparable Being of Yahweh.[1]

But Israel also transgressed in despising Yahweh's Holiness (22: 8) and in defiling His holy sanctuary (23: 38). Therefore, judged on her own merits, Israel is no more holy than the other nations. The exiles will survive, but this is due to no merit on their part. For Yahweh bids them 'Be ashamed and confounded' and in preserving them says, 'I do not this for your sake . . . but for mine holy name' (36: 32 and 22). Here, however, Yahweh is not merely concerned about His reputation or the opinion in which He may be held by the peoples of the world. For in Hebrew as well as in Babylonian thought[2] the term 'name' primarily means essence or existence. Hence, 'to know the name of a man is the same as to know his essence'.[3] When the Psalmist

[1] Cf. here S. H. Blank, H.U.C.A., 15, 1940, pp. 34 ff.
[2] George Contenau, *Everyday Life in Babylonia and Assyria*, p. 160.
[3] J. Pedersen, *Israel*, I–II, p. 245.

says of God, 'They that know thy name will put their trust in thee' (Ps. 9: 10) he means that they who know who God really is cannot but put their confidence in Him. The same thought is evident in the words, 'Our heart shall rejoice in him, because we have trusted in his holy name' (Ps. 33: 21). Similarly, 'the place which Yahweh . . . shall choose . . . to put his name there' (Dt. 12: 5) is the place which Yahweh Himself will actually inhabit. Likewise when the Israelites were told to 'hew down the graven images' of the heathen gods and to 'destroy their name out of that place' (Dt. 12: 3) they were in effect commanded to destroy the existence of these gods. This identity of Yahweh with His name is further exemplified in passages in which Yahweh is represented as acting through His name. In Psalm 20: 1 we read:

> The Lord answer thee in the day of trouble,
> The name of the God of Jacob set thee up on high;

while again in Isaiah 30: 27 we read, 'Behold the name of Yahweh cometh from afar, burning with his anger and in thick rising smoke'. In such contexts 'name' is invested with the attributes of the divine personality and expresses the character and being of God.

Ezekiel also frequently uses the word 'holy' in association with the name of Yahweh (e.g., 20: 39; 36: 20, 22; 39: 7, 25). Deriving from a root (קדש) signifying 'separation' or 'apartness',[1] the term holy is primarily used of Yahweh in the Old Testament. 'Holy, holy, holy, is the Lord of hosts: the whole earth is full of his glory' is the definition of God which we find in Isaiah's vision in the temple (Is. 6: 3). In other places in the Old Testament the word is used as a synonym for Yahweh.[2] Thus in a passage in Hosea which implies a contrast in the attributes of God and man we read: 'I am God and not man; the Holy One in the midst of thee' (11: 9). Again Isaiah speaks of 'the law of the Lord of hosts and . . . the word of the Holy One of Israel' (5: 24), while Habakkuk addresses God as 'O Lord my God, mine Holy One'

[1] B.D.B., p. 871.
[2] Cf. N. H. Snaith, *The Distinctive Ideas of the Old Testament*, p. 42.

(1 : 12). In Isaiah 40: 25 we read, 'To whom will ye liken me, that I should be equal to him? saith the Holy One', and in a later context we read of the 'Holy One' as 'the Creator of Israel' (Is. 43: 15). Holy is therefore an attribute of Yahweh which expresses His transcendental, incomparable and divine nature: it is as Baudissin remarked, the 'characteristic of the whole being of God revealed in Israel, a connotation of all His unique qualities'.[1] When, then, Ezekiel speaks of God's 'Holy name' he but affirms the uniqueness and majesty of Yahweh in all His inexhaustible power and glory. And in view of the claims of the surrounding nations for their gods and of their attempts at depreciating the God of Israel (cf. 35, 13 ; 36: 20) it was this property of Yahweh which he now wished to emphasise. Moreover, when Yahweh is represented as acting for His 'name's sake' it is implied that He acts only as Yahweh can. He is bound by no external laws, yet He must be true to His own nature. If it were His purpose to redeem mankind by His election of the Israelites, then, in order that they should survive as a people, He had to bring them out of Egypt (20: 9–10), and again out of the wilderness (20: 17–22). On each occasion He 'wrought for' His own 'name's sake' so that He might express Himself and His purpose for mankind. Even obdurate Israel will eventually realise this; for in the restored and regenerated kingdom which Ezekiel later envisages the Israelite people will fully acknowledge Yahweh's sovereignty: 'And ye shall know that I am Yahweh, when I have wrought with you for my name's sake, not according to your evil ways, nor according to your corrupt doings' (20: 44). Far, then, from acting out of concern for His own reputation God rather acts so that men may ultimately gain redemption and grace from His actions.

A God who thus acts must therefore for Ezekiel be a just God; and it was this property of God which he now tried to impress upon the exiles. They must, however, first be reminded of the consequences of their own sins, for as representatives of the house of Judah they necessarily shared her guilt: 'You have gone the

---

[1] W. W. Baudissin, *Studien zur semitischen Religionsgeschichte*, Leipzig, 1878, 2, p. 79.

way of your sister; therefore I will give her cup into your hand. Thus says the Lord God: You shall drink your sister's cup which is deep and large; you shall be laughed at and held in derision, for it contains much; you will be filled with drunkenness and sorrow. A cup of horror and desolation, is the cup of your sister Samaria; you shall drink it and drain it out. ... Therefore thus says the Lord God: Because you have forgotten me and cast me behind your back, therefore bear the consequences of your lewdness and harlotry' (23: 31–35, R.S.V.). Ezekiel not only claimed that the exiles were justly punished but, further, argued for the justice of God by saying that if after the eventual fall of Jerusalem a few survivors were to arrive in Babylon, they would, by continuing in their sinful habits, convince them of the justice of God's acts: 'When you see their ways and their doings ... you shall know that I have not done without cause all that I have done in it, says the Lord God' (14: 23). It may be doubted, however, if he would have succeeded in his purpose of refuting their contention that 'the way of Yahweh is not just' as long as the exiles were thinking in terms of the nation and the community. For while the nation may have been justly brought to an end, the exiles were, nevertheless, suffering in some degree for this. But Ezekiel was not interested in vindicating God's righteousness from the standpoint of the Israelite nation. It was sufficient that the nation had come to an end, and that the old order was over. The exiles should adapt themselves to new circumstances and should not think of themselves as remanent members of a punished nation but as individuals. His immediate concern then was to persuade them of the rights of the individual and the value of the individual soul.

To this end Ezekiel expounds a doctrine as significant as it was novel. In direct contradiction of the belief that the sons suffer for the sins of the fathers (18: 2–3) he declares that the message of Yahweh is: 'Behold, all souls are mine; the soul of the father as well as the soul of the son is mine (18: 4) ... the son shall not suffer for the iniquity of the father, nor the father suffer for the iniquity of the son' (18: 20, R.S.V.). He forthwith applies the implicates of this doctrine to an individual case: 'If a man is righteous and does what is lawful and right, if he does not . . . oppress anyone, but restores to the debtor his pledge, commits no robbery, gives his bread to the hungry . . . withholds his hand from iniquity, executes true justice between man and man, walks in my statutes, and is careful to observe my ordinances, he is righteous, he shall surely live, says the Lord God' (18: 5–9, R.S.V.). Ezekiel then proceeds to consider the son of this righteous man: 'If he begets a son who is a robber, a shedder of blood, who does none of these duties, but . . . oppresses the poor and needy, commits robbery, does not restore the pledge . . . lends at interest, and takes increase, shall he then live? He shall not live . . . he shall surely die; his blood shall be upon himself' (18: 10–13, R.S.V.). He next considers the case of a son of this wicked man. 'But if this man begets a son who sees all the sins which his father has done, and fears, and does not do likewise, who does not . . . wrong anyone, exacts no pledge, commits no robbery, but gives his bread to the hungry . . . withholds his hand from iniquity . . . observes my ordinances, and walks in my statutes; he shall not die for his father's iniquity; he shall surely live' (18: 14–17, R.S.V.). Listening to his statement with some incredulity, the people remarked, 'Why should not the son suffer for the iniquity of the father?' To this the prophet replied: 'When the son has done what is lawful and right, and has been careful to observe all my statutes, he shall surely live' (18: 19). The far-reaching principle of individualism was thus established. And an important corollary to this principle is the doctrine of individual responsibility which Ezekiel enunciated thus: 'The righteousness of the righteous shall be upon himself, and the wickedness of the wicked shall be upon himself' (18: 20). Contrary to popular belief Yahweh has no 'pleasure in the death of the wicked' but would 'rather that he should turn from his way and live' (18: 23). God then deals with men as individuals and is not influenced by the sins or righteousness of a past generation. As a man is not affected by the guilt of others so also there can be no transfer to him of the merits of the righteous: 'though these three men, Noah, Daniel, and Job' were in a sinful land 'they should deliver but their own souls by their righteousness saith the Lord God' (14: 14). Ezekiel contended that if in the eyes of God a man is bad he will 'die'; if he is righteous he will 'live'.[1] Further, a man is free to determine the course of his own life, and may therefore renounce his past for good or ill. Neither is he necessarily tied and bound by the chain of his sins, for God is more ready to welcome the sinner back to righteousness than to condemn him in his wickedness: 'Therefore I will judge you, O house of Israel, every one according to his ways, says the Lord God. Repent and turn from all your transgressions, lest iniquity be your ruin' (18: 30, R.S.V.). Before, then, the exiles should pronounce on the justice of Yahweh they should first consider their own sins and negligences: 'O house of Israel, are my ways not just? Is it not your ways that are not just?' (18: 29, R.S.V.).

Ezekiel's statement of his case for the justice of God may not, of course, meet every consideration in the argument required for a modern establishment of theodicy. Certain inconsistencies may be observed in his presentation of divine retribution. Thus, if a wicked man turns from his evil and observes God's statutes 'he shall surely live, he shall not die' (18: 21); but on the other hand, however righteous a man may be, once he lapses into sin he shall die; 'none of the righteous deeds which he has done shall be remembered' (18: 24). Again in accordance with his postulate that the righteous shall save his soul it is implied in 14:14 f. that the righteous in Jerusalem would be preserved in the doom of the city, yet in 21: 4 Yahweh is represented as saying: 'Because I will cut off from you both righteous and wicked, therefore my sword shall go out of its sheath against all flesh from south to north.' This indiscriminate treatment of all alike is somewhat contrary to the prophet's doctrine of individual retribution. Moreover, considerations of heredity, environment, and other factors which together constitute for the individual the problem of evil, were not adequately recognised.[2] Certain aspects of the problem were

[1] Cf. G. A. Cooke, op. cit., p. 195.
[2] Cf. A. S. Peake, *The Problem of Suffering in the Old Testament*, 1904, pp. 24–25; G. A. Cooke, op. cit., p. 196; W. A. Irwin, *The Old Testament: Keystone of Human Culture*, New York, 1952, p. 211.

raised by Ezekiel's older contemporary, Habakkuk, when he asked, 'Art not thou from everlasting, O Lord my God, my Holy One? ... Thou who art of purer eyes than to behold evil and canst not look on wrong, why dost thou look on faithless men, and art silent when the wicked swallows up the man more righteous than he?' (Hab. 1: 12–13). Recognition of God as a righteous and not as an arbitrary omnipotent being thus prompted the question as to why the righteous should suffer.[1] What, however, emphasised the problem of evil was the fact that Yahweh seemed indifferent although 'the wicked swallows up the man more righteous than he'. But although raising a most perplexing and abiding question Habakkuk's only comment towards solving the difficulty was 'The righteous shall live by his faith' (2: 4).[2] Jeremiah, as we have seen, was not unaware of the problem, but being of a deeply religious nature rather than of a speculative mind, he found a solution in the absolute surrender of himself to the service and will of God.[3] With the deterioration of the national circumstances the problem became accentuated for many of the Hebrew people;[4] and now the exiles openly declared 'The way of Yahweh is not just'. Ezekiel was concerned to meet this situation and to establish that, in contrast to the 'unjust ways' of the house of Israel, Yahweh' 'ways' were 'just' (18: 25). But his arguments as preserved in the present book strictly refer only to a refutation of the notion that the sons suffered for the sins of the fathers. It is true he stressed that the righteous shall save his soul alive; but this, again, was strictly in relation to the state of the soul when man came to his judgment and is scarcely applicable to the suffering which a man may experience though leading a blameless life. This aspect of the problem is later discussed in the book of

[1] Cf. Walter Eichrodt, *Man in the Old Testament* (Eng. trans.), Lond., 1951, pp. 56–58.
[2] See here Oesterley and Robinson, *Hebrew Religion*, 1944, pp. 265–266.
[3] 'The emphasis with Jeremiah is on personal religion, with Ezekiel on personal responsibility' (A. S. Peake, op. cit., p. 27).
[4] It is doubtful if I. I. Mattuck is right when he says, 'The fact is that suffering did not present a problem in the thought of the prophets' (*The Thought of the Prophets*, Lond., 1953, p. 137). W. A. Irwin on the other hand remarked, 'One of the acute problems that engrossed biblical thought was what we call the problem of evil' (*The Old Testament: Keystone of Human Culture*, p. 99). See also N. K. Gottwald, *Studies in the Book of Lamentations*, S.C.M., Lond., 1954, pp. 48–52.

Job, although even here no solution is offered beyond the implication that mortal man cannot fathom the incomprehensibility of the divine nature and purpose. But although Ezekiel did not deal directly with the problem of evil his emphasis on the responsibility of the individual marks a profound advance on the approach to the problem. For whatever difficulties are connected with this question, the individual must not for that reason disclaim all responsibility for the misfortunes he experiences, or the evil he observes, in life.

Apart from religious and moral considerations Ezekiel's emphasis on individualism was a particularly timely message to the exiles at this period.[1] Deported from their native land with its communal pattern of life and settled in different centres of Babylonia, it is doubtful if they would have survived for long as a racial entity if they did not adapt themselves to more individualistic conditions of life. Development of their particular lot or holding called for individual effort, while opportunities for participation in the commercial activities of Babylonia were at first available to individuals only. The advantages to be gained from the establishment of commercial businesses in this land gradually became evident to the exiles and in turn stimulated individualistic enterprises amongst them.[2] A life, moreover, which was lived in the midst of an old and advanced civilisation had the effect of inciting particular reactions and responses. The individual Israelite was thus induced to make decisions for himself and to accept or reject elements of his environment in accordance with his own judgment.

It was similar in regard to worship. The communal worship at the central sanctuary was no longer possible; and although communities governed by elders now met for purposes of prayer, the worship of Yahweh was perforce a matter of the individual conscience. The more, therefore, the individual Israelite was encouraged to think and act for himself, the sooner could he 'make' within him 'a new heart and a new spirit' (Ezek. 18: 31)

[1] Cf. here R. C. Dentan, *Interpretation*, 5, 1951, pp. 157–158.
[2] Cf. J. M. Powis Smith, *Amer. Jour. of Theol.*, 10, 1906, pp. 261–263.

8

and discover the secret of personal fellowship with God. If, moreover, the religion of Israel were to survive it could only do so through individual exiles.

But doubt and despondency occasionally seized them and they could still say, 'Our bones are dried up, and our hope is lost; we are clean cut off' (37: 11). Ezekiel consequently assured them that their situation would not always be as the present. For, though he himself regarded the destruction of the nation necessary, he also believed in the restitution of the Israelite people in Palestine. The exiles may be downcast, but they must remember that God promised life, not death or despair. Pondering over the words of the exiles he at length becomes convinced that Yahweh could unite and vivify even scattered bones which lacked the coherence of skeletons. The belief thus engendered is verified through his vision of the valley of dry bones (37: 1–2): 'Son of man, can these bones live? And I answered, O Lord God, thou knowest. Again he said to me, Prophesy to these bones, and say to them, O dry bones, hear the word of the Lord. . . . Behold, I will cause breath to enter you, and you shall live. . . .' (37: 3–5, R.S.V.). Ezekiel then describes with dramatic power the miraculous integration of the dismembered bones and the gradual appearance of sinews, flesh and skin, 'but there was no breath in them' (37: 8). Yahweh, however, said, 'Prophesy to the breath, . . . and say . . . Thus says the Lord God: Come from the four winds, O breath, and breathe upon these slain, that they may live.' Ezekiel then continues, 'So I prophesied as he commanded me, and the breath came into them, and they lived, and stood upon their feet, an exceedingly great host' (37: 9–10). The revivification of these bones represents the resuscitation of the national life of Israel: 'Son of man, these bones are the whole house of Israel. . . . Therefore prophesy, and say to them, Thus says the Lord God: Behold, I will open your graves, and raise you from your graves, O my people' (37: 11–12, R.S.V.). It is significant, however, that as the bones, though integrated and covered with sinews and flesh, had no life in them until the breath was breathed upon them, so the Israelites though raised from their graves are not regarded as being aware of the divine activity until God endows them with His spirit: 'And I will put my spirit within you, and you shall live, and I will place you in your own land' (v. 14).

The Israelites will not only be restored to their own land but they will no more be divided into two kingdoms. Their unity is symbolised by the joining of one stick representing Judah with another representing Israel (37: 16–17): 'And when your people say to you, Will you not show us what you mean by these? say to them, Thus says the Lord God: Behold, I am about to take the stick of Joseph . . . and I will join with it the stick of Judah, and make them one stick . . . say to them, Thus says the Lord God: Behold, I will take the people of Israel from the nations . . . and bring them to their own land; and I will make them one nation in the land . . . and they shall be no longer two nations, and no longer divided into two kingdoms' (37: 18–22, R.S.V.). But divine, rather than monarchical government will be a characteristic of the restored nation. To some extent the exiles 'were scattered because there was no shepherd' (34: 5). Instead, then, of rulers who neglected the charge of their flock (34: 2, 8). Yahweh will be the shepherd of His sheep: 'For thus says the Lord God: Behold, I, I myself will search for my sheep, and will seek them out. . . . I will rescue them from all places where they have been scattered . . . and will bring them into their own land; and I will feed them on the mountains of Israel . . .' (34: 11–13).

In this theocratic state Yahweh will make 'a covenant of peace' (34: 25) with His people. For although Israel had broken the covenant (16: 59) which God had earlier made with her (16: 8) yet, through His mercy and grace, He would now enter into a new relationship with her. The pre-exilic prophets believed that God's punishment inflicted by the hands of the nations would achieve the purification of His people;[1] but from his experience with the exiles Ezekiel realised that captivity and exile would not in itself effect the conversion of the sinful. Dispersion and captivity may have destroyed the pride in the nation and rendered

[1] Cf. G. E. Wright, *God Who Acts*, Lond., 1952, pp. 53–54.

the individual susceptible to the word of God, but only God's grace could ultimately create a new spirit and a new heart. Man is, however, called upon to exert considerable effort in attaining his own salvation: 'Repent and turn from all your transgressions. . . . Cast away from you all the transgressions which you have committed against me, and get yourselves a new heart and a new spirit' (18: 30–31, R.S.V.). But man's own striving is of no avail without the redemptive activity of God:[1] 'For I will . . . bring you into your own land. I will sprinkle clean water upon you, and you shall be clean from all your uncleanness, and from all your idols I will cleanse you . . . and I will take out of your flesh the heart of stone and give you a heart of flesh. And I will put my spirit within you, and cause you to walk in my statutes . . . and you shall be my people, and I will be your God' (36: 24–28, R.S.V.). In this passage Ezekiel preaches a message similar to that of Jeremiah's doctrine of the New Covenant. Lustration is to be the agent of Yahweh's cleansing. By this He declares His Forgiveness, and then by implanting 'a new heart . . . and a new spirit' He enables man to attain Regeneration. Further, it is by the grace of God rather than by his own efforts that man recognises and acknowledges his faults: 'Then you will remember your evil ways, and your deeds that were not good; and you will loathe yourselves for your iniquities and your abominable deeds' (36: 21, R.S.V.). So much indeed does Ezekiel attribute to the redemptive activity of God that it seems St. Paul was influenced by his teaching when at a later date he said: 'For God has done what the law, weakened by the flesh, could not do: sending his own Son in the likeness of sinful flesh . . . in order that the just requirement of the law might be fulfilled in us, who walk not according to the flesh but according to the Spirit. . . . To set the mind on the flesh is death, but to set the mind on the Spirit is life and peace' (Rom. 8: 3–6, R.S.V.).[2] Ezekiel as well as St. Paul realised that the knowledge of God implanted in man's

---

[1] Cf. here the teaching of Article X, '. . . Wherefore we have no power to do good works, pleasant and acceptable to God, without the grace of God by Christ preventing us. . . .'

[2] Cf. A. B. Davidson, *The Theology of the Old Testament*, 3rd impress., 1907, p. 343.

heart alone enables him to see and acknowledge his faults, and in the light of this new experience he can but loathe and condemn his former self.

Judged, then, in terms of his age Ezekiel's teaching marks a significant advance in the history of Hebrew religious thought. Called to the office of a prophet in Babylon, he had to deal with the many problems experienced by his fellow exiles there. He had to dissuade them from regarding their exile as an indication that Yahweh had been unable to protect His land or His people. The surrounding nations may be derisive of Israel, but Yahweh was still active and would eventually visit them with retribution. For Yahweh was not only aware of the historical changes which were passing over the Near East but even the powerful Nebuchadrezzar was but a servant in His hand. The God of Israel would yet vindicate His Holiness and sovereignty in the eyes of all the nations. Neither would the exiles be abandoned by Him, but they must learn that He deals with men in accordance with their individual acts. This stress on individualism and on the sacredness of the individual soul enabled the exile to satisfy his religious quests midst the confusion and uncertainty of the temporal scene. But equally important for the assurance and enrichment of the spiritual life was Ezekiel's declaration of the atoning grace of God in effecting the salvation of man.

VI

THE MESSAGE OF DEUTERO-ISAIAH

ABOUT a generation after Ezekiel there arose in the exile a prophet whose utterances represent the most sublime concepts in all Hebrew thought and theology. The name of this prophet is unknown, but his message is contained in chapters 40–55 of the present book of Isaiah. Since the work of Duhm[1] these are generally recognised as forming a unity and as deriving substantially from one author. Two divisions may, however, be recognised within this unity: one, comprising chapters 40–48, and the other chapters 49–55. Chapters 40–48 presuppose a situation prior to the fall of Babylon. The Jews are in captivity in the land of the Chaldeans (42: 22, 24; 48: 20): Cyrus has entered on the stage of history (44: 28; 45: 1); he has made rapid conquests in the east and north-west (41: 2–3, 25; 46: 11) and is about to challenge and overthrow the power of Babylon (48: 14; 46: 2). These allusions to his progress indicate that the Persian has overwhelmed Astyages the Mede, and has also defeated Croesus of Sardis and therefore suggest that the prophet was active in the decade before the fall of Babylon in 539.[2] The historical situation as represented by chapters 49–55 is on the other hand somewhat different. The absence of a reference to Cyrus seems to imply that Bayblon has already fallen to his armies. Although in 48: 20 we hear the summons: 'Go ye forth of Babylon, flee ye from the Chaldeans', the actual liberation of the Jews is not yet effected (49: 8–9). Nevertheless, 'the captive exile shall speedily be loosed' (51: 14), and we later read, 'Depart

---

[1] *Das Buch Jesaia*, Gött., 1892 (4th edn., 1922).

[2] Cf. Sidney Smith, *Isaiah, Chapters XL–LV*, Schweich Lectures, 1940 (Lond., 1944), pp. 22, 36, 52; R. H. Pfeiffer, *Intro. to the Old Test.*, pp. 456–7; A. Bentzen, *Intro. to the Old Test.*, 1952, pp. 104–105.

ye, depart ye, go ye out from thence' (52: 11). A restoration of Zion is also envisaged (52: 1–6); tidings to this effect are being published (51: 7–10) and songs of rejoicing shall be sung in the city that was desolate (54: 1 f.). Such considerations, then, combine to suggest that the contents of chapters 49–55 may be assigned to the year 538 or shortly afterwards.

Some scholars, however, deny that different historical circumstances may be recognised in chapters 40–55 and regard them together with chapters 56–66 as forming an essential unity; while the Roman Catholic scholar E. J. Kissane[1] is prominent amongst those who defend the traditional claim that the entire 66 chapters of the present book were written by the eighth-century prophet, Isaiah the son of Amoz. Most scholars who argue for the unity of chapters 40–66 find little difficulty in placing their composition in the exilic period.[2] But in 1928 C. C. Torrey propounded the view that chapters 40–66 were written, not by a prophet of the exile, but by one who lived in Palestine in the late fifth century.[3] The reference to Cyrus and Babylon were, he claims, inserted by an interpolator who was influenced by the Chronicler's fiction of the exile,[4] and 'With the half-dozen slight but potent touches removed' (p. 38) we have the work as it left the hands of its fifth-century author. In 1948 W. A. Elmslie was able to accept 'the validity of Torrey's contentions' and accordingly expressed the view 'that in Isa. xxxiv, xxxv, xl–lxvi, *for the most part* we have to do with a single, profoundly spiritual, Prophet'.[5] More recently U. E. Simon, declared himself as being 'convinced' of the essential soundness of Torrey's arguments and said that 'The real Isaiah . . . ought to be placed . . . at about 400 B.C.'[6] It must be admitted, of course, that no one is more sensitive to the spiritual value of the contents of Isaiah 40–66 than Torrey. Throughout his *Second Isaiah* he extols the work of

[1] *The Book of Isaiah*, vol. 2, Dublin, 1943.

[2] E.g., W. F. Albright, *The Archaeology of Palestine and the Bible*, 1932, p. 218; F. James, *Personalities of the Old Testament*, 1939, p. 363; L. Finkelstein, *The Pharisees*, vol. 2, pp. 627–631; cf. also G. A. Smith, *The Book of Isaiah*, vol. 2 (new edn., 1927), pp. 21 f.

[3] *The Second Isaiah*, pp. 104–110.   [4] Pp. 38–52.

[5] *How Came Our Faith*, p. 343.

[6] *A Theology of Salvation: A Commentary on Isaiah XL–LV*, Lond., 1953, p. 16.

'one of the greatest men of antiquity' (p. 39); and on page ix he could say, 'In the soundness and scope of its religious philosophy it stands alone in the literature of the ancient world, while in the wealth of its formal beauties it is unapproached by any other Hebrew writing.' He regrets that the division of the prophecies into Second and Third Isaiah detracted from the sublimity of their composition (pp. 1–19) and declares that one of the 'results' of regarding such prophecies as a work of 'the Babylonian exile' was 'to transform the sublime poetry of a seer into a somewhat bizarre fantasia on current events' (p. viii). Although concerned only with chapters 40–55 somewhat similar considerations prompted Simon to say that 'Since Isaiah cannot be the author of unwittingly great predictions but only of real prophecy we must reject out of hand any setting, background, or date which would belittle the part he played intentionally as a prophet.'[1] Applying this criterion to the circumstances of the Jews in exile in about 540, he remarks that 'this prophecy amounts to so much enthusiastic nonsense if it had been originally addressed at that time to those people. Then the prophecy is a ludicrous failure' (p. 16). Simon regards the period of about 400 B.C. as a suitable time for the prophet's activity 'when he broadly and deliberately attacks the narrow schools of Judaism and the Paganism of the Greek world and invites all, Jews and Gentiles, in Palestine and everywhere to accept salvation on a transcendental scale' (ibid.).

Yet, apart from internal considerations, it may well be doubted if the late fifth century as maintained by Torrey, or later as maintained by Simon, provides any more likely background for these prophecies, or that their delivery in the exilic age would amount to 'a bizarre fantasia on current events' or 'enthusiastic nonsense'. Although the end of the fifth, and early fourth, century was the age of Socrates and Plato it could scarcely boast of the same widespread intellectual activity as that of the sixth century, and would therefore have been less likely to provoke or to demand the expositions and declarations characteristic of the utterances of the Second Isaiah. For the sixth century was a period of intellectual

[1] Op. cit., p. 15.

awakening such as man had never experienced before, nor indeed was it equalled again till the age of the Reformation in the Christian era. It was an age when among the Greeks tradition and superstition were yielding to the rudiments of scientific inquiry, when, disregarding the beliefs of inherited cosmogonies, Thales and Anaximander were speculating on the origin and nature of the universe. It was, moreover, the period when vital religious movements spread over the ancient world. Zoroaster had refined the traditional Iranian beliefs and conceived of his God Ahura-Mazda in the most exalted and ennobling terms. The Buddha rejected the elaborate ceremonial of the Brahmans and regarded the search for truth as the essential concern of man. In addition startling and significant events were taking place on the political scene. The supremacy of the Egyptian and Semitic races, enjoyed since the dawn of history, was about to succumb to the pressure of the Indo-European peoples who were descending on the plains of Asia Minor and Mesopotamia. And casting nostalgic glances on the past, as if conscious that their civilisations had run their courses, the Egyptians and the Babylonians relinquished their hold on the ancient world. Hence issuing from the fastnesses of their mountain homes, the Medes and Persians, united into a formidable power by Cyrus, were about to enter the strongholds of the last Neo-Babylonian king and assume the leadership of the Near East. It was this universal ferment of thought and this surge of political forces that formed the background of the prophecies of Deutero-Isaiah, and it was this age in turn which makes his utterances so significant. For consider how critical the situation had become for Israel: the nation had been dismembered, her people disillusioned and the survival of her race threatened. If, then, one of her prophets could not have measured the intellectual problems of the age in relation to his own conception of Yahweh, her religion too, would have succumbed before the new impetus in Near Eastern thought.

But independently of such considerations the internal evidence of the text points to the exilic age as the period in which Deutero-Isaiah lived. Apart altogether from what Torrey calls 'The

Cyrus-Babylon Interpolations' there are passages which denote that the prophet was referring to a contemporary figure of the exilic scene. Thus in chapter 41 : 2-3 we read : 'Who stirred up one from the east whom victory meets at every step? He gives up nations before him, so that he tramples kings under foot; he makes them like dust with his sword, like driven stubble with his bow. He pursues them and passes on safely, by paths his feet have not trod.' Torrey interprets this passage as referring to Abraham (pp. 310 f.) although the tenses defining the activity of the person in question do not suggest a reference to a person in the past. Moreover, in verse 25 we read that this same figure will not only 'trample on rulers as on mortar' but, 'will call' (יקרא) on the name of Yahweh. Again it is difficult to see how the use of such tenses could be applicable to a past figure. But as Simon remarked, 'The facts also are not quite accurate: Abraham did not set out nor, indeed, arrive as a conqueror.... The identification collapses completely when Abraham is forced to assume the rôle of the fulfiller of history, as here.'[1] Simon cannot, however, see in these passages a mere reference to 'military success' (p. 71), but rather an eschatological reference to the activity of 'God's Messiah' (p. 72). But an essential requisite of the prophetic message was that of intelligibility, and it is doubtful if any Jewish audience would have interpreted the above passages as a reference to Abraham or have seen in them even a vague reference to the activity of the Messiah. Moreover, if these verses were intended by their author to refer to Abraham it is curious that he is not mentioned by name as in verse 8, as there would have been no need to refer to him in the veiled language of the text. Indirect references would, however, have been sufficient to the Jews at this juncture of events to identify the unnamed person as Cyrus. Hence as Sidney Smith remarked, 'Only one interpretation would have been possible to a contemporary', that of recognising in these passages a reference to Cyrus who was now preparing to invade certain Babylonian provinces.[2] It would have been equally difficult for an audience to see in chapter 45 : 1-4 a reference to

---

[1] Op. cit., p. 70.   [2] *Isaiah, Chapters XL-LV*, p. 51.

anyone other than a successful military leader. This is clear even
if with Torrey we omit the words 'to Cyrus' in the first verse:
'Thus saith Yahweh to his anointed . . . whose right hand I have
grasped, to subdue nations before him and ungird the loins of
kings, to open doors before him that gates may not be closed . . .
I will break in pieces the doors of bronze and cut asunder the
bars of iron' (vv. 1–2). The subjugation of nations, the opening
of doors of brass, the severing of iron bars is a veritable description
of the irresistible march and rapid conquests of a powerful army.
Moreover, the consideration that Yahweh could say of this person, 'I call you[1] by your name, I surname you, though you do
not know me' (v. 4) implies that the person in question was a
non-Israelite outside the historical and religious sphere of Israel.
And, apparently conscious of this, Torrey does not identify this
person with Abraham, but with the Servant in the capacity of
'the Messianic leader'.[2] Commenting on this passage, Simon says,
'The real explanation, if not found in the fraudulent addition to
the text, should be sought in typology', and continues, 'Remini-
scence creates types. . . . No wonder, then, that the conqueror of
. . . Babylon, Cyrus, was also remembered as a type. Though
working over a century after his victories, Isaiah can use his name
which fits into his historical symbolism and suits his general
purpose of calling back the Dispersed' (p. 128). This is tantamount to acknowledging that there is a reference in this passage
to Cyrus, but in accordance with the late date which he has
adopted for its composition Simon would account for the
reference by resorting to the expedient of typology. The figure
who is mentioned in verses 1–4 of chapter 45 is again obviously
referred to in verse 13: 'he shall build my city and set my exiles
free'. In harmony with his interpretation of verses 1–4 Torrey
also sees here a reference to the function of the Servant of Yahweh
(p. 360), while Simon would interpret the verse as indicating the
achievement of 'the Creator's Messianic intervention' (p. 132).
Yet while there were Jews in the Dispersion long after the sixth

[1] Omitting the conjunction Waw and reading אקרא as a parallel to אכנך as R.S.V.,
and as indeed with Torrey, op. cit., pp. 238, 358.
[2] Op. cit., pp. 358, 147.

century, at no time after the fall of Babylon would it be correct to regard them as being in captivity as here stated. The only historical background which can explain the implications of this verse is that provided by the entry of Cyrus into Babylon and his subsequent issue of an edict enabling the Jews to return to Palestine.

This same historical period is also presupposed in the reference to the Babylonian gods, Bel and Nebo, in chapter 46: 1: 'Bel bows down, Nebo stoops, their idols are on beasts and cattle; these things you carry are loaded as burdens on weary beasts.' Torrey suggests that there might here be a reference to the collapse of the Persian rule at the close of the fifth century (p. 128). Simon is more definite in assigning the passage to this period, remarking that 'Bel and Nebo had come toppling down from the Babylonian pantheon' (p. 141) and concludes: 'It follows, therefore, that Isaiah could not have spoken or quoted this oracle in the sixth century' (p. 142). Such an interpretation could, however, be maintained only if we assume that these gods did literally 'come toppling down from the Babylonian pantheon'; but the text denotes nothing more than a reference to the impotence of these gods in contrast to the omnipotence of Yahweh. Bel and Nebo are mentioned, because, as we know from a contemporary Babylonian document, they were the chief gods of the Babylonian pantheon in the sixth century B.C.[1] But reference to them could have significance only if they were still the acknowledged heads of the gods; and the inference to be drawn from the text is, that even in the summit of their splendour they were insignificant before the incomparable Yahweh. The prophet had probably in mind the occasion of the new Year Festival when these gods were taken in procession through the streets of Babylon and had to be carried as burdens on weary beasts. And if a literal interpretation is sought for the words 'they themselves go into captivity' it is probably to be found in the fact that prior to the fall of Babylon Nabonidus ordered the removal of many gods from the suburbs

[1] The Cyrus Cylinder in which Cyrus is represented as saying: 'May all the gods whom I have resettled in their sacred cities ask daily Bel and Nebo for a long life for me' (A.N.E.T., p. 316).

to places of safety within the city.[1] For, 'calling a bird of prey from the east' (46: 11)[2] Yahweh will direct him against Babylon and effect the subjugation of the city, as chapter 47 shows. According to Simon this chapter is concerned with 'the great ethical problem of retribution' and 'occurs here in a Babylonian context' because 'the theme of vengeance is a favourite one in the Old Testament' and the various powers including 'Babylon ... must perish'.[3] Addressing himself to this chapter Torrey says 'that Babylon was for the prophet and his fellow countrymen the typical embodiment of the worldly power and pride which he declares to be fleeting'. The prophecy, however, 'is not a *vaticinium ex eventu*, nor was it even written at a time when *the city* seemed to be threatened; on the contrary ... she was at this time in the full enjoyment of prosperity and apparent security, and with no threatening cloud on the horizon' (p. 368). If this is, however, the Babylon of the Persian period how are we to account for the phrase 'O daughter of the Chaldeans' occurring in verses 1 and 5? It surely appears here only because the prophet is referring to the Babylon of the Chaldean rule. The city may still be in the full enjoyment of her powers, yet scarcely 'with no threatening cloud on the horizon' for Cyrus, 'the bird of prey', is already poised to attack this 'mistress of kingdoms'. Babylon may consult 'those who divide the heavens, who gaze at stars, who at new moons predict what shall befall' her (47: 13); but 'there is none to save' (47: 15) from the irresistible onslaught of Cyrus. For as stated in 48: 14, 'Yahweh loves him; he shall perform his purpose on Babylon, and his arm shall be against the Chaldeans.'[4]

[1] Cyrus Cylinder, line 33 (A.N.E.T., p. 316); cf. here R. W. Rogers, *Cuneiform Parallels to the Old Testament*, p. 393; also J. Skinner, *Isaiah XL–LXVI* (Camb., 1917), pp. 76–77.

[2] Torrey changes the עַיִט (bird of prey) of the text to עַבְדִי (my servant) (op. cit., p. 366), although the word is used of Nebuchadrezzar in Jer. 49: 22; Ezek. 17: 3. Simon accepts the text but thinks it represents 'the Messiah ... as a destroying vulture' (op. cit., p. 144). [3] Op. cit., p. 150.

[4] Or 'against the seed of the Chaldeans' reading וּבְזֶרַע for וּזְרֹעַ. It will be observed that although retaining the words 'Babylon' and 'Chaldea' in 47: 1, 5 Torrey rejects them in 48: 14, in a context which has an obvious reference to Cyrus (op. cit., p. 377). Simon accepts the authenticity of these words here, but again interprets them typologically (pp. 155 f.) and connects the loved one of the text with Israel (pp. 159–160).

A sufficient number of passages have been considered to show the relevance of the prophecies of Deutero-Isaiah to the events connected with the conquests of Cyrus and the fall of Babylon.[1] Similar passages and considerations point to Babylonia as being the place where the prophet delivered these prophecies. According to Torrey 'Their author wrote in Palestine, presumably in Jerusalem, near the end of the fifth century B.C.' (p. 53); while Simon, regarding the prophet as a sort of itinerant preacher, writes, 'His aim was to enrol disciples and to this end he delivered his message in many places. He would be a welcome speaker in the synagogues of the land and of the Diaspora' (p. 21). Many scholars, while accepting the exilic date for the prophet, do not, however, place his activity in the exile. Thus Phoenicia or the Lebanon has been proposed by Duhm and Causse,[2] Egypt by Ewald[3] and Hölscher,[4] while Torrey has not been alone in his advocacy of a Palestinian scene for the prophet's ministry. J. A. Maynard,[5] Moses Buttenwieser,[6] George Dahl[7] and L. Finkelstein[8] have all contended that the Second Isaiah worked in Palestine. Like Torrey (p. 53) these writers maintain that the prophecies bear no trace of a Babylonian environment. Thus Buttenwieser wrote: 'As a final proof that Deutero-Isaiah did not write in Babylonia it may be pointed out that while in Ezekiel there is abundant evidence of his Babylonian background, in Isaiah 40–55 there is nothing to suggest that the writer was living in Babylonian surroundings.'[9] This statement may be taken as representative of the advocates of a Palestinian locale for the activity of the prophet. But as G. A. Smith pointed out, 'The absence of local colour from our prophecy has been greatly exaggerated. We find . . . break after break of Babylonian light and shadow falling across our path—the temples, the idol-manufacturers, the processions of images, the diviners and

---

[1] Cf. here Sidney Smith, *Isaiah, Chapters XL–LV*, pp. 49–75, 183–193.
[2] A. Causse, *Les dispersés d'Israel*, Paris, 1929, p. 35.
[3] *History of Israel*, 5 (Lond., 1874), p. 42.   [4] *Die Propheten*, pp. 321, 373.
[5] 'The Home of Deutero-Isaiah', J.B.L., 36, 1917, pp. 213–224.
[6] 'Where did Deutero-Isaiah Live?', J.B.L., 38, 1919, pp. 94–112.
[7] 'Some Recent Interpretations of Second Isaiah', J.B.L., 48, 1929, pp. 362–377.
[8] *The Pharisees*, 2, pp. 627, 631.   [9] Op. cit., p. 100.

astrologers, the gods and altars especially cultivated by the characteristic mercantile spirit of the place; the shipping of that mart of nations, the crowds of her merchants, the glitter of many waters, and even that intolerable glare, which so frequently curses the skies of Mesopotamia (xlix, 10).'[1] A consideration of one or two passages will serve to verify the significance of these words.

The prophet shows his familiarity with Babylonian life in his references to the Babylonian idols (40: 19, 20; 44: 9–20; 45: 20) and to the astrology and necromancy (47: 12–13) practised there; while his observations on the reclining postures of Bel and Nebo being carried about on beasts indicate that both he and his audience had witnessed such scenes more than once. Moreover, the oracle against Babylon appears to have been delivered in the city itself. In imperious yet personal tones he addresses her thus: 'Come down and sit in the dust, O virgin daughter of Babylon; sit on the ground without a throne, O daughter of the Chaldeans' (47: 1). The taunts which follow are those of a bystander familiar with the stately features of the city and the languor of her people: 'take the millstone and grind meal, put off your veil . . . for you shall no more be called the mistress of the kingdoms' (vv. 2–5). To her tired inhabitants, frantic as to the fate of the future, he observes, 'You are wearied with your many counsels' (v. 13), and he further reminds them that their astrologers and prognosticators 'are like stubble . . . they cannot deliver themselves from the power of the flame' (v. 14). The contention that the prophet was in Babylon when he delivered this oracle is further strengthened by another passage in which, on what must have been the eve of the return, he addresses his fellow exiles with the words, 'Go ye forth of Babylon, flee ye from the Chaldeans' (48: 20).[2]

---

[1] *The Book of Isaiah*, 2 (new edn., 1927), pp. 13–14.

[2] As a further indication that the prophet delivered his oracles in Babylon some scholars have drawn attention to the similarity of the language of Deutero-Isaiah (41: 13; 42: 6) to that of the Cyrus Cylinder (e.g., line 12; A.N.E.T., p. 315). Cf. R. Kittel, 'Cyrus und Deutero-Isaiah', Z.A.W., 18, 1898, pp. 149–162; O. C. Whitehouse, 'The Historical Background of Deutero-Isaiah', *Expositor*, 89, 1893, pp. 110–111; W. Rudolph, Z.A.W., N.F., 2, 1925, p. 105, n. 2; F. Stummer, 'Einige Keilschriftliche Parallelen zu

While, however, we may assign the prophecies of Deutero-Isaiah to a Babylonian background in the period of the exile, it is questionable if their compilation as preserved in Isaiah 40–55 is the work of their author. It is doubtful if they are compiled in chronological order as no great unity of subject matter is to be recognised in their present arrangement.[1] Certain great themes are discernible throughout the work, and some relating to the incomparable nature of Yahweh are repeated in order to emphasise the importance of that concept. Like his predecessors, Deutero-Isaiah seems to have uttered his oracles as occasion required, but the collection of these oracles and their compilation into book form seem to have been the work of disciples of the prophet.[2] We have no reason, however, to doubt the genuineness of most of the material of the book or to conclude that the figure and personality of the prophet are lost in the loftiness of his thought. It is true we do not know his name, but there is a reference to his call in 40: 6–8, expressed in language typical of the prophet, in which the earthly and ephemeral nature of man is contrasted with the eternal and abiding word of God. Some scholars have seen in the biographical material of 49: 1–6 and 50: 4–9 references to Deutero-Isaiah himself: thus such expressions as, 'Yahweh ... made my mouth like a sharp sword' (48: 2), 'I have set my face like a flint and I know that I shall not be put to shame' (50: 7) and 'For Yahweh helps me ... he who vindicates me is near' (50: 7–8) have been regarded as autobiographical.[3] This is, of course, equivalent to the identification in these passages of the prophet himself with the Suffering Servant. It must, however, be

---

Jes. 40–66', J.B.L., 45, 1926, pp. 171–189. As such inscriptions were written after the fall of Babylon it is scarcely likely that Deutero-Isaiah was influenced by them. The similarity of language suggests, however, that both prophet and scribe used the common court language of the day.

[1] Cf. Pfeiffer who says, 'It is in vain that one looks for logical sequence and arrangement in his poems. ... In his rushing flow of words, in his passionate outbursts, a few identical great thoughts and hopes reappear constantly without rational order ...' (*Intro. to the Old Test.*, p. 465). James Muilenburg, however, is of the opinion that 'there are no repetitions because of the numerous fresh combinations and contexts in which the specific title appears' (*The Interpreter's Bible*, V, 1956, p. 400).

[2] Cf. Sidney Smith, op. cit., pp. 20–23.

[3] E.g., Sidney Smith, op. cit., pp. 19, 186, 189.

admitted that such passages remind us of the opposition which Jeremiah, and indeed Ezekiel, experienced; and Deutero-Isaiah's portrayal of the Servant in certain contexts might well be drawn from his own experience as a prophet.

Although we are in possession of but little evidence relating to the prophet's life we are in no doubt as to his place amongst the great prophets of Israel. He assumes his office conscious of the significance of the historical events amid which he is called. Recognising that a new age, fraught with tremendous consequences for mankind, was being inaugurated he represents Yahweh as saying: 'Behold, the former things have come to pass, and new things I now declare' (42: 9). And confident of the realisation of these things he thus addresses the exiles: 'Comfort, comfort my people, saith your God' (40: 1). For although the Jews enjoyed a fair degree of material prosperity they were, nevertheless, still in exile; and as exiles they must have experienced some feelings of isolation and strangeness in the great city of Babylon with its place and influence among the nations of the world.[1] But compared with Yahweh 'the nations are like a drop from a bucket': they 'are as nothing before him, they are accounted by him as less than nothing and emptiness' (40: 15–17). 'Princes' too shall be brought 'to nought' and 'the rulers of the earth' become 'as nothing' (40: 23). Potentates and tyrants are powerless before Yahweh and Israel has nothing to fear from them: 'Behold, all who are incensed against you shall be put to shame and confounded; those who strive against you shall perish . . . those who war against you shall be as nothing at all. For I, Yahweh your God, hold your right hand; it is I who say to you, Fear not, I will help you' (41: 11–14). But the exiles are not confident of this and impatient of their captivity cry: 'My way is hid from Yahweh and my right hand is disregarded by my God' (40: 27, R.S.V.). The prophet accordingly informs them that God is not only mindful of their particular lot but, since the

---

[1] In his *Cyropaedia* (V, ii, 8) Xenophon refers to 'all the wealth of Babylon', while Sardis is 'the richest city in Asia, next to Babylon' (VII, ii, 11). (The Loeb Classical Library, 1914.)

9

beginning of time He has been cognisant of the circumstances and designs of all the races of the earth. For Yahweh initiates and controls history: 'Have you not known? Have you not heard? Yahweh is the everlasting God, the Creator of the ends of the earth. He does not faint or grow weary' (40: 28). Rather He has been active in history 'calling the generations from the beginning' (41: 4). It was He who called Abraham and 'took' Israel 'from the ends of the earth' (41: 8–9). Empires may rise and fall and Israel may be involved in the vicissitudes that follow but Yahweh's purpose will not be frustrated. The rising power of Persia is but the instrument of His will inasmuch as it will contribute to the realisation of the 'new thing',[1] the liberation of the exiles and their march homewards. The exiles, however, seem to question the propriety of the role which a non-Hebrew might play in their deliverance. They were still conscious of their national pride and thought of their own liberators of the past. But Cyrus and his place in history were also within the providence of God. All peoples of the earth were alike made by God and, although Israel was called by Him for a special reason, He may use any nation for the furtherance of His purpose as a potter may fashion to his will the clay in his hands. Israel can therefore hardly question the designs of her Creator and Sustainer: 'Woe to him who strives with his Maker, . . . Does the clay say to him who fashions it, What are you making? . . . Thus says the Lord, the Holy One of Israel, and his Maker: Will you question me about my children, or command me concerning the work of my hands? . . .' (45: 9 f., R.S.V.). Neither need the exiles have any foreboding that deliverance by Cyrus would involve subservience to him. On the contrary deliverance will be entirely due to God's grace and providence: Cyrus 'shall build my city and set my exiles free, not for price or reward says Yahweh of hosts' (45: 13). The peoples of the nations too are invited to consider the significance of current events (41: 1). Before an international audience Yahweh asks, 'Who stirred up one from the east whom victory meets at

---

[1] Cf. C. R. North, 'The "Former Things" and the "New Things" in Deutero-Isaiah' in *Studies in Old Testament Prophecy*, pp. 111–126.

every step? He gives up nations before him, so that he tramples kings under foot ... He pursues them and passes on safely. ... Who has performed and done this ...?' (41 : 2–4). But although eminently successful in his conquests Cyrus is unconscious of the purpose he is serving : 'For the sake of my servant Jacob and Israel my chosen, I call you by your name, I surname you though you do not know me, I am Yahweh and there is no other' (45 : 4–5). He who has been 'declaring the end from the beginning, and from ancient times things not yet done' (46 : 10) will now vindicate His purpose in the eyes of the world and can assure Israel 'I give men in return for you, peoples in exchange for your life' (43 : 4, R.S.V.).

Yahweh's control of history derives ultimately from His entire sovereignty over nature. For He is responsible for all creation. It was He who 'laid the foundation of the earth', who 'spread out the heavens' and caused them to assume their ordered place in the universe (48 : 13): it was He who 'measured the waters in the hollow of his hand ... enclosed the dust of the earth in a measure and weighed the mountains in scales and the hills in a balance' (40: 12). The prophet's emphasis on the creative and cosmic activity of Yahweh sharply distinguishes his view of creation from others obtaining in the ancient Near East. According to the Babylonian cosmogony as represented in the epic *Enuma Elish* the primal principles were the male Apsu and the female Tiamat.[1] At length Tiamat predominates and becomes the personification of primeval 'chaos'. The god Marduk then appears and slays Tiamat. From her split body he forms heaven and earth, the element water being assumed to have been already in existence.[2] The belief that water was the primal substance was also held by Homer who spoke of 'Oceanus from whom the gods are sprung'.[3] Similarly Thales, the first of the Milesian philosophers, regarded 'water as the material cause of all things'.[4] There is likewise a reference to a pre-existent watery chaos in the

---

[1] Tablet I, lines 1–5 (A.N.E.T., pp. 60–61).
[2] Tablet IV, lines 137–140 (A.N.E.T., p. 67).
[3] *Iliad*, XIV, 201, 241.   [4] John Burnet, *Early Greek Philosophy*, p. 42.

cosmogony of Genesis I: 'In the beginning of God's creating
the heaven and the earth, the earth being chaos and confusion
(תהו ובהו tohu wabohu) and darkness upon the face of the Deep
(תהום Tehom) . . .'[1] Jeremiah too seems to have thought that the
world received ordered form from chaos and confusion, for in a
vision which purports to be a description of the earth abandoned
by God he says, 'I saw the earth, and lo, it was chaos and confusion (tohu wabohu), and the heavens and they had no light . . .'
(Jer. 4: 23). In Deutero-Isaiah, however, there is no implication
of a pre-existent chaos constituting the substance from which the
world assumes ordered existence. It is true we find a reference to
the cosmogonic myths in 51: 9: 'Was it not thou that didst cut
Rahab in pieces, that didst pierce the dragon?' Here, however,
Yahweh is only credited with a triumph which is ascribed to
Marduk in Babylonian mythology and to another deity in
Ugaritic mythological texts.[2] But while for purposes of apologetics Deutero-Isaiah may use such language he rejects any conception of chaotic matter as being pre-existent to Yahweh's
creation of the world. Rather, Yahweh 'created the heavens . . .
formed the earth and made it, he established it, he did not create
it a chaos (לא תהו בראה), he formed it to be inhabited' (45: 18). He
therefore conceives of Yahweh's creative activity as operating
prior to the appearance of any primeval matter. Other deities may
succeed only in making a chaos, but Yahweh's creation is purposeful and habitable. Of course Zoroaster said of Ahura-Mazda
that it was he 'who appointed the course of the sun and stars . . .
who sustained the earth . . . and the sky . . . who fashioned the
waters and the planets' who fashioned 'physical bodies' and did
'infuse life-breath into mortal bones . . .'[3] Admirable as this view
of creation is, it has not because of the dualism inherent in
Zoroastrianism the same emphasis on first principles which we

[1] So on grammatical grounds most moderns translate. Cf. H. Wheeler Robinson,
Inspiration and Revelation in the Old Testament, p. 19; W. A. Irwin, *The Old Testament:
Keystone of Human Culture*, New York, 1952, p. 69.

[2] See J. A. Montgomery and Z. S. Harris, *The Ras Shamra Mythological Texts*, Philadelphia, 1935, pp. 39 ff. and 78 ff.; C. F. A. Schaeffer, *The Cuneiform Texts of Ras Shamra-
Ugarit* (Schweich Lectures), Lond., 1939, pp. 65–66.

[3] Yasna 44, parts of verses 3, 4, 5 and Yasna 31, 11.

find in Deutero-Isaiah nor is it expressed, as the prophet's is, with a consciousness of refuting the notion of creation out of existing chaos. Nor was Deutero-Isaiah's view of creation that of a development from an impersonal monism as conceived by the contemporary Greek philosopher Anaximander. According to Theophrastus Anaximander held that 'the material cause and first element of things was the Infinite' that it was 'neither water nor any other of the so-called elements, but a substance different from them which is Infinite from which arise all the heavens and the worlds within them'.[1] This Infinite was 'ageless and eternal' and Anaximander thought that by a process of abstraction from it and subsequent differentiation all things came into being.[2] While such speculation represents an advance on earlier Greek cosmogonic concepts it was not a view of creation which could be acceptable to the prophet. For this was a monistic conception of creation while his was profoundly theistic. Yahweh alone is the eternal Being 'the Creator of the ends of the earth' (40: 28). It was He who 'stretched forth the heavens and laid the foundations of the earth' (51: 13): it was He who 'made all things' (44: 24).

Yahweh not only created the universe but also that which 'comes from' the earth and 'gives breath to the people upon it' (42: 5). He is therefore the Sustainer as well as the Creator of all life upon earth. Moreover the elements of His creation respond to His bidding: 'Shower, O heavens, from above, and let the skies rain down righteousness; let the earth open, that salvation may sprout forth, and let it cause righteousness to spring up also; I Yahweh have created it' (45: 8). He can command the deep 'be dry' (44: 27) and 'set in the desert the cypress' (41: 19) and make 'a way in the sea, a path in the mighty waters' (43: 16). He can assert this unlimited power over nature because, having 'made all things', He continues to control them.

It follows that Yahweh who is 'the Everlasting God, the Creator of the ends of the earth' (40: 28) is the only God. The question as to when monotheism appeared in Israelite thought

[1] Burnet, op. cit., p. 54.   [2] Burnet, op. cit., p. 66.

has been keenly discussed in recent years. W. F. Albright has been a prominent exponent of the traditional view that Moses conceived of Yahweh in terms of exclusive monotheism,[1] while this claim has been no less vigorously denied by other scholars.[2] It must be remembered that in view of the nature and date of the Pentateuchal documents, upon which we are dependent for our information about Moses, we have no reliable means of ascertaining the particular concept of God which he entertained in the thirteenth century B.C. No one would doubt the intensity of his belief in Yahweh, 'yet the most probable view is that the notable contribution of Moses did not consist of the discovery and dissemination of a belief in a single God of all the world'.[3] It is even doubtful if our records relating to the activities of Elijah and Elisha allow us to attribute to them anything more than a view of Yahweh as the national God of Israel. When, however, we come to the utterances of the writing prophets we are enabled to assess the nature of their theological presuppositions with greater confidence; and we find that the notion of monotheism had some place in their conception of Yahweh.[4] Thus Amos, the first of these prophets, declared that Yahweh's punishment will extend over Damascus and 'the strongholds of Ben-Hadad' (Amos 1:3–4) and also over the neighbouring kingdoms (1–2:2). Indeed Yahweh could exert His power even farther afield: 'Are ye not like the Ethiopians to me, O people of Israel says Yahweh, Did I not bring up Israel from the land of Egypt, and the Philistines from Caphtor, and the Syrians from Kir?'

---

[1] *From the Stone Age to Christianity*, pp. 196–207; J.B.L., 67, 1948, pp. 379 f. F. James (*Personalities of the Old Testament*, p. 32), G. E. Wright (*The Old Testament against its Environment*, pp. 30–41), and John Bright (*Interpretation*, 5, 1951, p. 7) are amongst those who share the view of Albright. Cf. also C. A. Simpson who in his discussion of 'The Beginnings of Yahvism' (*The Early Traditions of Israel*, Oxford, 1948, pp. 419–425) said: 'Momentary monotheism was a characteristic of primitive Yahvism from the first, necessary because of the very nature of the religion' (p. 425).

[2] E.g., T. J. Meek, 'Monotheism and the Religion of Israel,' J.B.L., 61, 1942, pp. 21 f.

[3] W. A. Irwin, *The Old Testament: Keystone of Human Culture*, p. 25.

[4] Speaking of the emergence of 'monotheism' from the Hebrew 'national religion', the Jewish writer I. I. Mattuck recently remarked: 'It dictates a belief in the progressive revelation of God, and attests the evolutionary process in religion, that monotheism was the result of a development; the Prophets had been prepared for it by the preceding religious development of the Hebrews' (*The Thought of the Prophets*, pp. 45–46).

(Amos 9: 7). Isaiah not only conceived of Yahweh as passing judgment on the state of Syria (Is. 7: 4, 8) but actually of using the great power of Assyria to accomplish His own ends (Is. 10: 5–6). Jeremiah was confident that Yahweh would bring a nation 'from the north' against Judah and that He could also send the king of Babylon against Moab, Edom and other western states (Jer. 27: 1–8). In the mind of Ezekiel Yahweh was no less powerful. The great powers of Egypt and Tyre as well as the smaller neighbouring states would all suffer at the hand of Nebuchadrezzar as Yahweh's avenging agent. All these prophets then assumed that Yahweh's power was effective outside Israel and that He had complete control of even the most powerful Near Eastern nations. Yet such assertions emphasise Yahweh's extensive power rather than state that He alone exists as God. We must read the utterances of Deutero-Isaiah before we hear the question, 'Is there a God beside me?' and the categorical denial, 'Yea ... I know not any' (44: 8); and again we read, 'I am Yahweh and there is none else; beside me there is no God' (45: 5). Thus for the first time in Hebrew literature we meet with the definitive statement that Yahweh alone has claim to deity and that consequently He alone is God (cf. also 43: 13).

The precise etymological meaning of the term YHWH is a question upon which scholars have long debated. The traditional interpretation of the term as 'He Who Exists' or 'He Who causes to be' are still maintained by some scholars,[1] but attempts have also been made to see in the word the meaning of 'The Blower', 'The Speaker', 'The Revealer', 'The Destroyer', and 'The Sustainer'.[2] Perhaps one of the most suggestive treatments of the question in recent years has been that by Julian Morgenstern[3] in which he argues that the term אני יהוה (Ani YHWH) as used by Deutero-Isaiah is his characteristic designation of the

---

[1] E.g., W. F. Albright, *From the Stone Age to Christianity*, p. 198.

[2] For recent discussions of the question, see, R. A. Bowman, 'Yahweh The Speaker', J.N.E.S., 3, 1944, pp. 1–8; W. A. Irwin, 'The Tetragrammaton', J.N.E.S., 3, 1944, pp. 257–259; Julian Obermann, 'The Divine Name YHWH in the Light of Recent Discussion', J.B.L., 68, 1949, pp. 301–323; E. Schild, 'I Am That I Am', V.T., 4, 3, 1954, pp. 296–302.

[3] 'Deutero-Isaiah's Terminology of the Universal God', J.B.L., 62, 1943, pp. 269–280.

universal and eternally existent One. He further draws attention
to the fact that the term אני יהוה (Ani YHWH) is paralleled by
another recurring phrase אני הוא (Ani Hua) and concludes that
הוא (Hua) is synonymous with, and is therefore another title for,
יהוה (YHWH).[1] This parallelism is evident in passages such as
the following:

> 'I Yahweh, the first and with the last, I am He' (41 : 4).[2]
> '. . . that you may know and believe Me
> and understand that I am He' (43 : 10).
> 'I am God, and also henceforth I am He' (43 : 13).

It will be noticed that these passages are in contexts in which the
prophet is concerned to deny existence to other gods and by
contrast asserts the eternal divinity and power of Yahweh.
Similarly, in 42 : 8 considerable significance is attached to the
fact that Yahweh is the name of the prophet's God with the
implication that certain properties are His which cannot be
attributed to idols: 'I am Yahweh, that is my name; my glory I
give to no other, nor my praise to graven images.' Whatever,
then, is the true philological derivation of the term YHWH it is
clear that for Deutero-Isaiah, it connoted a Being who is eternal
and omnipotent and whose attributes can be predicated of Him
alone.

The circumstances of the time explain why the prophet was
at such pains to represent Yahweh in exclusively monotheistic
terms. The exiles were in the greatest city of the world of their
day and must therefore have been witnesses to the conflict of
thought arising from the meeting of many cultures and customs
in this cosmopolitan city. In this environment they must have
heard something of the cosmological speculations which were now
characteristic of Ionian and Iranian thought. From the seventh
century onwards the Greeks had been extending their relationships with the outside world; and the Weidner tablets record that
Greeks and Lydians as well as Egyptians and other peoples were

---

[1] Cf. also S. H. Blank, 'Studies in Deutero-Isaiah', H.U.C.A., 15, 1940, pp. 14–18.
[2] Cf. B.D.B., p. 216b (5).

in Babylon in the early sixth century. Significant also is the mention of Medes and Persians on these tablets;[1] but that there were at this time Medes and Persians in Babylon besides those under the care and control of the royal household, as the tablets suggest, may be seen from the following considerations. After the fall of Harran in 610 the Medes dominated northern Mesopotamia till 555.[2] Nebuchadrezzar had in the meantime become master of Babylon, but he was too preoccupied with his campaigns against Tyre and Egypt to turn his attention to the Medes: rather, it is probable that he remained on good terms with his allies at Carchemish. Indeed he is reported to have had a Median consort and to have constructed the 'hanging gardens' in her honour;[3] and it is likely that many other Medes were attracted to the wonders of the city of Babylon. The internal dissensions which prevailed in Babylon after his death in 562 would serve as a further inducement to some adventurous Medes to migrate there. Moreover, when Nabonidus ascended the throne one of his first acts was to form an alliance with Cyrus[4] encouraging thereby associations between the Babylonians and Persians. The Persians gradually occupied the territory surrounding Babylon from 547 onwards,[5] and during this period, Nabonidus himself being absent in Arabia, many of them must have penetrated to Babylon. From 610, then, till the fall of Babylon there were many opportunities for infiltrations of both Medes and Persians into the capital of the Babylonian empire. And under such circumstances it is probable that Zoroastrianism which had been promulgated as a faith in 588 had been known in Babylon when Deutero-Isaiah was preaching there some forty years later.

In addition to the medley of thought and belief which would thus be introduced into Babylon the exiles were also exposed to the pretentious claims which were being made on behalf of the

[1] A.N.E.T., p. 308b.
[2] Cf. Sidney Smith, *Isaiah, Chapters XL–LV*, p. 27; A. T. Olmstead, *A History of the Persian Empire*, p. 37.
[3] E. Herzfeld, *Archaeological History of Iran* (Schweich Lectures, 1934), Lond., 1935, p. 27.
[4] A. T. Olmstead, op. cit., pp. 36–37; Sidney Smith, op. cit., pp. 32–33.
[5] Sidney Smith, *Isaiah, Chapters XL–LV*, p. 40; *Babylonian Historical Texts*, pp. 108–109.

gods of Babylon. Further, the Babylonians themselves were at
this time approaching the study of the phenomena of the heavenly
bodies in a more methodical manner with the consequent development of the science of astrology.[1] The rustic Hebrew who had
believed from of old that Yahweh had certain powers over nature
might well wonder if his national God of Israel had any control
over the illimitable universe as disclosed by the new and astonish-
ing science. But, however perplexing the situation may have been
for the exiles, it only provided Deutero-Isaiah with an opportunity
of addressing himself to them in the capacity of an apologist.[2] He
did not deny, but rather accepted, the immensity of the universe
as disclosed by the emergent physical sciences; for by relating
such discoveries to the creativity and providence of God he
adduced them as evidence for the uniqueness of Yahweh. The
Babylonians may regard the stars and the planets as self-existent
bodies possessing some mysterious powers over the lives of men;
but Deutero-Isaiah contends that contemplation of these bodies
can only lead to the conviction that their creation is the feat of
Yahweh. Inasmuch as Yahweh called 'them all by name' He is
responsible for their individual and continued existence; for
according to the Babylonian 'Doctrine of the Name' nothing
exists unless it has a name.[3] It is therefore against this background
of Babylonian thought that we hear the prophet say: 'Lift up
your eyes on high and see; who created these? He who brings
out their host by number, calling them all by name; by the greatness of his might, and because he is strong in power not one of
them is missing' (40: 26). Nor were the effects of this declaration
in any way vitiated by the contemporary speculations of the

---

[1] W. A. Irwin, *The Intellectual Adventure of Ancient Man*, p. 249.

[2] 'It is important to realise that Second Isaiah wrote with conscious realisation of the
problem of apologetics; he took up the issue specially and of set purpose' (W. A. Irwin,
The Intellectual Adventure of Ancient Man, p. 251). Cf. here also L. Finkelstein, who
observed that 'The ferment in religious faith evident everywhere in the world . . . and
. . . the confusion of doctrine observable in western cities, together with the international
situation' caused by the appearance of Cyrus, 'offered an unexampled opportunity for a
widespread religious movement which Israel might initiate' (*The Pharisees*, 2, pp. 470–
471).

[3] George Contenau, *Everyday Life in Babylonia and Assyria* (700–530 B.C.), p. 160.

Ionians; for if the beginnings of natural philosophy were drawing attention to the unified structure of the universe and the mysterious properties of the natural elements the prophet could point to these observations as but another indication that the universe was the creation of a single purposeful mind: 'Who has measured the waters ... marked off the heavens with a span, enclosed the dust of the earth in a measure ... Who directed the Spirit of Yahweh or ... instructed him? Whom did he consult for his enlightenment?' (40: 12–14). The impressive pattern discernible in the physical universe is, moreover, to be attributed to Yahweh who claims: 'My hand laid the foundation of the earth, and my right hand spread out the heavens; when I call to them they stand forth together' (48: 13). By appealing therefore to considerations which in modern thought might be termed the cosmological and teleological arguments, Deutero-Isaiah established the claim of Yahweh as the supreme and sole Creator, and it is significant that throughout his prophecies he resorts to the force of these arguments with singular frequency (e.g., 40: 22; 51: 13). The prophet could, however, carry his arguments further; for in addition to creating the universe of old and maintaining the planets in their set courses Yahweh could suddenly intervene in this ordered course of nature. He could 'make the rivers a wilderness' (50: 2) or 'the wilderness a pool of water' (41: 18) so that people 'may see and know and consider and understand ... that the hand of Yahweh has done this' (41: 20).

In accordance with this sustained theme of his argument it is to some purpose that Deutero-Isaiah repeatedly asks, 'To whom ... will ye liken God?' (40: 18, 25; 46: 5). The Babylonian environment naturally suggests an idol. But an idol is made by a workman who is himself created by God (54: 16). Sometimes, indeed, the making of an idol is but a mere afterthought: if after cooking his food and warming himself by the fire a man has still some wood left he may decide to make an idol (44: 15–17). This practice the prophet rightly attributes to ignorance and superstition: 'No one considers, nor is there knowledge or discernment' to realise that it is but falling 'down before a block of wood' (44: 19). Such a man 'feeds on ashes; a deluded mind has led him astray, and he cannot deliver himself or say, Is there not a lie in my right hand?' (44: 20). Elsewhere the prophet remarks, 'They have no knowledge who carry about their wooden idols and keep on praying to a god that cannot save' (45: 20). The idols which are fashioned out of gold and silver are equally impotent. Bel and Nebo, the most revered gods in Babylon, were thus fashioned but their helplessness was pitiable to behold. Yahweh could justly claim 'I have made, and I will bear; I will carry and will save' (46: 4); but dumb and lifeless Bel and Nebo were 'loaded as burdens on weary beasts. They stoop, they bow down together, they cannot save the burden, but themselves go into captivity' (46: 2). How pathetic that man, bound to tradition and superstition, is unable to realise that an idol 'cannot move from its place' or that 'if one cries to it, it does not answer or save him from his trouble' (46: 7). But in addition to worshipping wooden idols and gods of gold and silver, the Babylonians had from their 'youth' been preoccupied with 'enchantments' and 'sorceries', and were 'wearied with' the 'many counsels' of 'those who divide the heavens, who gaze at the stars' and 'at the new moons predict' the future (47: 12–13). It is, however, only in vain that these astrologers and prognosticators try to wrest from the heavens the course of future events, for when God's judgment will fall on Babylon these people will be 'as stubble . . . they cannot deliver themselves from the power of the flame' (47: 14).

In true apologetic fashion the prophet continues his polemic against the idols. He examines their claims to deity, contrasts them with the properties of Yahweh, and so exposes their pretensions and confounds their worshippers. The temporality of the heathen gods contrasts sharply with the eternity of Yahweh. Not only were the idols fashioned by smiths and carpenters, but in the Babylonian Epic of creation we read that there was a time 'When no gods whatever had been brought into being, uncalled by name, their destinies undetermined.'[1] The Greek writer Hesiod also informs us in his *Theogony* that the gods were created from

[1] Enuma Elish, Tablet I, lines 7–8, as trans. in A.N.E.T., p. 61

chaos.[1] While such heathen gods were themselves created from existing matter within temporality Yahweh could say: 'Before me no god was formed, nor shall there be any after me' (43 : 10); 'I, Yahweh, the first and with the last; I am He' (41 : 4). Again, in contrast to a 'god that cannot save' (45 : 20) Yahweh 'is a just God and a Saviour' (45 : 21), and, unlike the idols which must themselves be carried, Yahweh 'does not faint or grow weary. . . . He gives power to the faint, and to him who has no might he increases strength' (40: 28–29). In their lifeless impotence the idols fail to give any demonstrable sign of divinity and so Deutero-Isaiah now challenges them to the test of prophetic utterance:[2] 'Set forth your case says Yahweh; bring your proofs, says the king of Jacob. Let them bring them, and tell us what is to happen. Tell us the former things, what they are, that we may consider them, that we may know their outcome; or declare to us the things to come. Tell us what is to come hereafter, that we may know that you are gods; do good, or do harm, that we may be dismayed and terrified' (41 : 21–23, R.S.V.). The 'former things' of verse 22 probably relate to the early victories of Cyrus,[3] and an appeal is made to the gods to interpret the significance of these events for the course of future history. Yahweh himself could claim: 'I stirred up one from the north, and he has come, from the rising of the sun, and he shall call on my name; he shall trample on rulers as on mortar, as the potter treads clay' (v. 25). The argument satirically continues, 'Who declared it from the beginning, that we might know, and beforetime, that we might say, He is right? There was none who declared it, none who proclaimed, none who heard your words' (v. 26, R.S.V.). In view of such silence and dumbness the only possible conclusion is: 'Behold they are all a delusion; their works are nothing; their molten images are empty wind' (v. 29). In contrast to the silence and impotence of the idols Yahweh is able to point to the realisation of His own predictions of past events and can also confidently

---

[1] Lines 901–903.
[2] Cf. S. H. Blank, 'Studies in Deutero-Isaiah', H.U.C.A., 15, 1940, pp. 1–6.
[3] So C. R. North, ibid., pp. 120–122, 126.

foretell the future: 'I am Yahweh, that is my name ... Behold, the former things have come to pass, and new things I now declare; before they spring forth I tell you of them' (42: 8–9). Yahweh is not, however, dependent merely on prediction of events to establish His claim to sole deity. He has infallible prescience only because it is He who determines and directs the course of world events: 'Remember this and consider, recall it to mind you transgressors, remember the former things of old; for I am God and there is no other; I am God, and there is none like me, declaring the end from the beginning and from ancient times things not yet done, saying, My counsel shall stand, and I will accomplish all my purpose, calling a bird of prey from the east, the man of my counsel from a far country. I have spoken, and I will bring it to pass; I have purposed, and I will do it' (46: 8–11, R.S.V.). It is therefore futile to conceive of a power or force in opposition to Yahweh, for a Being who possesses such absolute purpose of mind and will can execute with precision what He purposes: 'The former things I declared of old, they went forth from my mouth and I made them known; then suddenly I did them and they came to pass' (48: 3). It is because such things come to pass that the prophet is justified in appealing to the Israelites themselves in support of his arguments. The idols of the nations have neither prophets nor hearers (41: 26); 'their witnesses neither see nor know' (44: 9). But Yahweh has both the prophets and people of Israel as witnesses to His power and grace through the centuries: 'Let all the nations gather together, and let the peoples assemble. Who among them can declare this, and show us the former things? Let them bring their witnesses to justify them, and let them hear and say, It is true. You are my witnesses, says Yahweh' (43: 9–10). In contrast to the powerless and speechless gods of the nations who fail to produce either evidence or witnesses of a claim to deity Yahweh says: 'I declared and saved and proclaimed, when there was no strange god among you; and you are my witnesses' (43: 12).

Having, then, demonstrated the dumb impotence of the idols and successfully refuted their claims to deity, Deutero-Isaiah proceeds to enunciate some positive doctrines concerning the nature and person of God. Self-existent and independent of His creation (40: 22) Yahweh is 'the God of the whole earth' (54: 5). He is free and self determining: He will 'work and who can hinder it?' (43: 13). Of His creative word He says, 'It shall not return to me empty, but it shall accomplish that which I purpose, and prosper in the thing for which I sent it' (55: 11, R.S.V.). Yahweh's ways are inscrutable; 'his understanding is unsearchable' (40: 28); He says to man: 'My thoughts are not your thoughts, neither are your ways my ways. . . . For as the heavens are higher than the earth, so are my ways higher than your ways and my thoughts than your thoughts' (55: 8–9). He is omnipotent and takes counsel of no one (40: 14) and can execute all His designs (46: 10). It is pointless therefore to question His intention or His power: 'Is my hand shortened, that it cannot redeem? or have I no power to deliver?' (50: 2). He can make the unique claim, 'I have made, and I will bear; I will carry and will save' (46: 4). His immutability is to be contrasted with the changing and evanescent character of both man and nature: 'All flesh is grass. . . . The grass withers, the flower fades; but the word of . . . God will stand for ever' (40: 6–8). In like manner Yahweh could also say: 'The heavens will vanish like smoke, the earth will wear out like a garment, and they who dwell in it will die . . . but my salvation will be for ever, and my deliverance will never be ended' (51: 6, R.S.V.).

But, from their limited conception of history and world events, the Israelites had been inclined to doubt if Yahweh were really as powerful as the gods of Assyria and Babylonia.[1] It is reported of king Ahaz that after his defeat by the Syrians he set up a Syrian altar (2 Kgs. 16: 10 f.) and sacrificed 'to the gods of Damascus which smote him' saying, 'because the gods of the kings of Syria help them, therefore will I sacrifice to them that they may help me' (2 Chron. 28: 23). Similarly, the Judeans who survived the fall of Jerusalem and escaped to Egypt with Jeremiah openly declared their allegiance to the Assyrian goddess Ishtar on the

[1] Cf. A. B. Davidson, *The Theology of the Old Testament*, pp. 101 f.

grounds that when they worshipped her in the past they had a sufficiency of meat and drink. Accordingly, they defied Jeremiah thus: 'As for the word which you have spoken to us in the name of Yahweh, we will not listen to you. But we will do everything that we have vowed, burn incense to the queen of heaven and pour out libations to her, as we did, both we and our fathers, our kings and our princes, in the cities of Judah and in the streets of Jerusalem; for then we had plenty of food, and prospered and saw no evil. But since we left off burning incense to the queen of heaven and pouring out libations to her, we have lacked everything and have been consumed by the sword and by famine' (Jer. 44: 16–18). There were doubtless many exiles in Babylon in Deutero-Isaiah's time who thought as their kinsmen in Egypt (cf. Is. 40: 27; 49: 14; 50: 2). It had long been the prophetic view that Assyria and Babylon were but chastening instruments in the hands of Yahweh (Is. 10: 5 f.; Jer. 27: 8; Ezek. 29: 18–20) but in categorically denying the attributes of deity to the idols of the nations and in declaring that Yahweh alone is God, Deutero-Isaiah represents Him as being absolutely supreme over the destinies and movements of all the peoples of the earth. In comparison to the whole universe of His creation the nations are as 'drops' to a 'bucket', the isles insignificant, and the rulers of the earth but 'nothing' (40: 15, 23).

Yahweh, however, is not only lord of history and nature but His sovereignty extends over the entire psychical and moral spheres of life. We have noted that cosmological discussions were a feature of contemporary thought, that the Ionians were concerned with the search for the First Cause, and that Zoroastrianism accounted for the presence of good and evil in the world by the postulate of a Dualism of Light and Darkness. It is probable, however, that Deutero-Isaiah was not only acquainted with such speculations, but was also aware of the difficulties inherent in them; for he solved the Ionic problem of creation by claiming that Yahweh is the sole Creator and Controller of the universe, and the Zoroastrian problem of good and evil by his representation of Yahweh as Lord also of the realms whence moral and related problems arise: 'I am Yahweh and there is no other. I form light and create darkness, I make weal and create woe. I am Yahweh who do all these things' (45: 6–7, R.S.V.). His specific reference here to light and darkness as principles of good and evil suggests that it was prompted by the Persian belief that life is a tension between two distinct and opposing forces.[1] Hence, for the first time in the history of man's reflection on this problem, evil is itself attributed to a beneficent creator.[2] Earlier Hebrew prophets were faced with the problem and meditated as to its source, but now Deutero-Isaiah attributed it to the omniscient and omnipotent Yahweh. It was an original though bold concept. Yet, however attractive to pious minds the postulate of a dualism may be, it would be tantamount to acknowledging that God was opposed by a force as powerful as Himself. And according to the theology of Deutero-Isaiah God was the supreme and only Cause in the universe. He who created the earth, 'who giveth breath unto the people upon it, and spirit to them that walk therein' (42: 5) cannot in the last resource be excluded from the sphere of the sordid and evil. Yahweh 'created the ravager to destroy' (54: 16) and it was He 'Who gave Jacob for a spoil and Israel to the robbers' (42: 24). The problem of theodicy did not therefore arise in the thought of Deutero-Isaiah as for earlier prophets, for he was able to combine the concept of an omnipotent Creator with that of a just and righteous Ruler of the universe: 'I Yahweh speak the truth, I declare what is right' (45: 19); Yahweh is 'a just God and a Saviour' (45: 21) whose 'righteousness shall be for ever' and whose 'salvation' shall be 'unto all generations' (51: 8).

[1] Commenting on 45: 6–7 Sidney Smith remarked 'that these descriptions of YHWH, consonant with Hebrew faith, were . . . carefully composed for Cyrus to understand' (*Isaiah, Chapters XL–LV*, pp. 58–59). He seems to favour the view, however, that the prophet was referring to a tenet of Persian belief which was current before the official acceptance of Zoroastrianism, p. 156, n. 149. But see, G. E. Simcox, 'The Role of Cyrus in Deutero-Isaiah', *Jour. of American Oriental Society*, vol. 57, 1937, pp. 158–171.

[2] In Lam. 3: 38 we read, 'Is it not from the mouth of the Most High that good and evil come?' N. K. Gottwald regards all the poems of the book of Lamentations as 'stemming from the exilic period between 586 and 538 B.C.' (*Studies in the Book of Lamentations*, Lond., 1954, p. 21). With regard to chapter 3, however, Pfeiffer remarks that 'vv. 18–39 are commonplaces in the Psalter' and on good grounds places its author-ship in the third century (*Intro. to the Old Test.*, p. 723).

Indeed Israel's humiliation amongst the nations finds its explanation in Yahweh's justice and holiness. For although Yahweh had created all the peoples of the world He refers to Israel as 'my chosen people, the people whom I formed for myself that they might declare my praise' (43: 20–21). But Israel proved unworthy of her election: 'Thou hast not called upon me O Jacob ... thou hast been weary of me O Israel' (43: 22). She may 'swear by the name of Yahweh ... but not in truth, nor in righteousness' (48: 1). Hence, Yahweh says, 'I was wroth with my people, I profaned mine inheritance, and I gave them into' the 'hand' of Babylon (47: 6; cf. also 42: 24). But this gave Him no pleasure: 'O that you had hearkened to my commandments! Then your peace would have been like a river, and your righteousness like the waves of the sea' (48: 18, R.S.V.). Unfortunately, in common with the other nations, Israel was from the first prone to sin (43: 27) and manifested constant indifference to the word of God (48: 8). Yet for His 'name's sake' and His 'praise' Yahweh will not cut her off (48:9): 'for how should my name be profaned? My glory I will not give to another' (48: 11, R.S.V.). As therefore Yahweh 'formed' her for His 'servant' so He would now transform her (44: 21). This is, however, entirely an act of grace on Yahweh's part: 'For a brief moment I forsook you, but with great compassion I will gather you. In overflowing wrath for a moment I hid my face from you, but with everlasting love I will have compassion on you, says Yahweh, your Redeemer' (54: 7–8, R.S.V.). 'I, I am He who blots out your transgressions for my own sake, and I will not remember your sins' (43: 25); 'return to me for I have redeemed you' (44: 22).

Although Yahweh is the omnipotent creator, inscrutable in His Being, and lord of good and evil alike, He is yet a forgiving and personal God who invites the fellowship of His people: 'Seek Yahweh while he may be found, call upon him while he is near; let the wicked forsake his way, and the unrighteous man his thoughts; let him return to Yahweh ... for he will abundantly pardon' (55: 6–7). Only in such fellowship is there real life: 'Incline your ear, and come unto me; hear, that your soul may live' (55: 3, R.S.V.). It will be observed that this emphasis on the personality of God with whom life-giving fellowship may be experienced contrasts sharply with contemporary modes of thought which conceived of the ultimate reality in impersonal terms. Such fellowship could not, for example, be had with the impersonal ground of being conceived of by the Ionians, nor with the ultimate power postulated by the Buddha. For although Buddha enunciated a most noble moral code he doubted if any fellowship could be possible with an unseen being. According to Deutero-Isaiah, however, contemplation of nature should reveal the personal nature of the power behind the cosmic forces: 'Lift up your eyes on high and see: who created these . . .?' (40: 26). Similarly, reflection on the course of the world's history provides the answer to the question, 'To whom will ye liken God?' (40: 18). Moreover, Yahweh invites personal consideration of vital issues: 'Put me in remembrance; let us plead together; set forth thy cause that thou mayest be justified' (43: 26). Finally of His revelation of Himself and of His own nature Yahweh says: 'Draw near to me, hear this: from the beginning I have not spoken in secret, from the time it came to be I have been there' (48: 16, R.S.V.). Since existence itself Yahweh has performed acts which bespeak their divine origin. He has brought nature into being in all its impressive grandeur: He has authorised and brought to fulfilment the great events of history. He 'did not speak in secret in a land of darkness'; He 'did not say to the offspring of Jacob, seek me in chaos' (45: 19). The theogonies and legends of other deities associate them with chaos and confusion but Yahweh's acts may be discerned in the ordered, intelligible world, which in turn denote His creative, constructive and purposeful nature.

Yahweh not only reveals Himself to His people but He is constantly concerned for their welfare: 'I am Yahweh your God, who teaches you to profit, who leads you in the way you should go' (48: 17). The Babylonian gods are dumb and helpless and must themselves be carried, the Zoroastrian god is opposed by a force as powerful as himself, the Ionian principle of a first cause

is indifferent to personal needs, but Yahweh teaches and leads His
people. Nabonidus claimed to be 'the shepherd who fears his
god, honoured his command and obeyed it'.[1] But such a god has
proved ineffective and therefore non-existent. Of Yahweh alone
it can be said, 'He will feed his flock like a shepherd, he will
gather the lambs in his arms, he will carry them in his bosom,
and will gently lead those that are with young' (40: 11). He will
answer 'the poor and needy' the 'God of Israel will not forsake
them' (41: 17). Israel His chosen may be despised by the nations
but Yahweh can assure her, 'Fear not, for I have redeemed you;
I have called you by name, you are mine. When you pass through
the waters I will be with you; and through the rivers, they shall
not overwhelm you ... For I am Yahweh your God, the Holy
One of Israel, your Saviour' (43: 1–3). To those who 'know
righteousness' and 'in whose heart is' His 'law' His message is:
'Fear ye not the reproach of men, and be not dismayed at their
revilings' (51: 7). The fear of mortal man is but fleeting while
God's love is eternal and abiding: 'I, I am he that comforts you;
who are you that you are afraid of man who dies, of the son of
man who is made like grass, and have forgotten Yahweh, your
Maker...?' (51: 12).

As well as being immanent in His creation sustaining His
creatures and caring for the needy Yahweh is in addition active
as the Redeemer of souls. Only an omnipotent and universal God
is able to redeem: 'The Holy One of Israel is thy Redeemer, the
God of the whole earth shall he be called' (54: 5). This God of
the whole earth, in accordance with the universality of His Being,
offers redemption to the nations of the world; this 'just God and
a Saviour' pardons the ignorance by which the nations have
sinned and says, 'Look unto me and be ye saved, all the ends of
the earth' (45: 22). Ezekiel claimed that certain nations would
'know Yahweh', but only in acknowledgement of His power.
According to Deutero-Isaiah nations outside Israel will come
within the sphere of His universal salvation (55: 5). In the ulti-

---

[1] A. T. Clay, *Miscellaneous Inscriptions in the Yale Babylonian Collection*, New Haven,
1915, no. 45.

mate acknowledgement of Yahweh's sovereignty 'Every knee shall bow' and 'every tongue shall swear' (45: 23) and when Yahweh finally reveals Himself 'in the eyes of all the nations . . . all the ends of the earth shall see' His 'salvation' (52: 10).

Deutero-Isaiah was not, however, content to visualise the ultimate acceptance of God's salvation by all people but was deeply concerned with the historical realisation of this ideal. Accordingly the fulfilment of God's purpose is vested in a figure described in terms of a suffering Servant.[1] The question of the identity of the Servant has often been asked and variously answered. Attempts have been made to identify him with the nation Israel or a representative part of it, or again with a past or contemporary historical figure. Yet it is doubtful if any of these suggestions adequately represents the conception of the Servant as delineated in the Servant passages, for the actual realisation of his mission seems to lie beyond the compass of any of the figures suggested by such interpretations. It is rather probable that we must allow some fluidity of thought and interpretation to the concept that the Servant not only applies to Israel but to an ideal community within it, and also to an individual arising from that community. But whatever interpretation we attach to the concept it is clear that the mission of the Servant is to mediate God's salvation to the world. In 42: 1 Yahweh says of him: 'Behold my servant, whom I behold, my chosen, in whom my soul delights; I have put my spirit upon him, he will bring forth justice to the nations.' Similarly in the second Servant passage where the Servant himself is the speaker we read: 'Listen to me, O coastlands, and hearken, you peoples from afar. Yahweh called me from the womb, from the body of my mother he named my name. . . . And he said to me, You are my servant, Israel, in whom I will be glorified. . . . And now Yahweh says, who formed me from the womb to be his servant, to bring Jacob back to him, and that Israel might be gathered to him, for I am

[1] Is. 42: 1–4; 49: 1–6; 50: 4–9; 52: 13–53: 12. The Deutero-Isaianic authorship of these passages has been questioned, but there is an increasing tendency to regard them as the composition of the prophet himself. See C. R. North, *The Suffering Servant in Deutero-Isaiah*, Oxford, 1950, pp. 156–191.

honoured in the eyes of Yahweh, ... he says: It is too light a thing that you should be my servant to raise up the tribes of Jacob and to restore the preserved of Israel; I will give you as a light to the nations, that my salvation may reach to the end of the earth' (49: 1, 3, 5, 6, R.S.V.). Asserting his confidence in God, the Servant, in the third passage, says: 'I gave my back to the smiters, ... I hid not my face from shame and spitting. For the Lord God helps me; therefore I have not been confounded; therefore I have set my face like a flint, and I know that I shall not be put to shame; he who vindicates me is near. Who will contend with me? Let us stand up together. ... Behold, the Lord God helps me; who will declare me guilty? Behold, all of them will wear out like a garment; the moth will eat them up' (50: 6-9). Of course, in so far as suffering leads a sinner to reflection on his past it may have some value in recalling him to the ways of God.[1] Yet suffering and pain are amongst the great problems of life, and rarely has the sufferer in bearing his own burden brought people to God; a dejected and deformed appearance arouses but indifference in most people (cf. Is. 53: 2-3). But when it is known that suffering is borne for the sins of others, rather than for those of the sufferer himself, then, it may make some moral appeal to the hearts of men.

It was thus that the Servant suffered. 'He was despised and rejected by men; a man of sorrows, and acquainted with grief; and as one from whom men hide their faces he was despised, and we esteemed him not. Surely he has borne our griefs and carried our sorrows; yet we esteemed him stricken, smitten by God, and afflicted. But he was wounded for our transgressions, he was bruised for our iniquities...' (53: 3-5). This vicarious suffering had a redemptive value: 'Upon him was the chastisement that made us whole, and with his stripes we are healed ... the Lord has laid on him the iniquity of us all' (53: 5-6). He in whom 'there was no deceit' was 'stricken for the transgression of my people' (53: 8). Other Old Testament characters confessed their guilt in suffering (e.g., Ps. 38: 3-5, 17-18; Ps. 32: 3-5) or else

[1] Cf., e.g., Ps. 78: 34.

questioned God as to its justice (e.g., Ps. 44: 17–18; Jer. 15: 18; Job 34: 6), but in the Servant we have a unique instance in the Old Testament of suffering in silence.[1] This was because the Servant had a secret denied other mortals. Having no guilt of his own or no doubts of his God he was able to achieve what no other could. He was conscious of the grief he was enduring, but was conscious also that by it he was fulfilling the will and purpose of God. 'It was the will of Yahweh to bruise him; he has put him to grief; when he makes himself an offering for sin, he shall see his offspring, he shall prolong his days; the will of Yahweh shall prosper in his hand' (53: 10, R.S.V.). Yet out of this suffering and travail there emerges a sense of triumph and victory in the knowledge that he has enabled others to attain to righteousness: 'He shall see the fruit of the travail of his soul and be satisfied; by his knowledge shall the righteous one, my servant, make many to be accounted righteous' (53: 11). In making himself 'an offering for sin' he bore man's guilt thereby effecting for humanity the means of its restoration to God. But the Servant also has a place of honour in the restoration. For although the service of Yahweh involved suffering even 'to death' (53: 12) Yahweh could say of the Servant, 'He shall be exalted and lifted up, and shall be very high' (52: 13). And here we are reminded that when Christ came to do the will of God as no other could, 'He humbled himself and became obedient unto death, even on a cross. Therefore God has highly exalted him and bestowed on him the name which is above every name, that at the name of Jesus every knee should bow, . . . and every tongue confess that Jesus Christ is Lord, to the glory of God the Father' (Phil. 2: 8–11). Thus, whatever the concept of the Servant may have conveyed to the people of the prophet's day and later, the ideals embodied in it were only fully realised once in history.[2] The concept is in consequence all the more significant and represents the uniqueness of the prophet's teaching. For it shows

---

[1] G. A. Smith, *The Book of Isaiah*, vol. 2, p. 360.

[2] So C. R. North concludes his study of the question with the words, 'Original and Fulfilment join hands across the centuries' (*The Suffering Servant in Deutero-Isaiah*, p. 219)

that Deutero-Isaiah was not only concerned with Israel's mission to the nations of the world, but that in his inspired thought he spans the centuries to the time when the Advent of Christ gave full effect to his message of universal salvation.

CONCLUSION

The course, then, which we have followed in our discussion of the exilic age leads to the conclusion that the teaching of Deutero-Isaiah represents the most sublime expression of Hebrew religion as well as the most profound thought of his day. For in the sixth century B.C., when the ancient world was undergoing the most radical transformations of thought and power, Deutero-Isaiah could discern the hand of the God of Israel bringing to a decisive point a long succession of events which He controlled from eternity. The Semitic races which for nigh on a thousand years had held undisputed authority over the ancient Near East were now becoming subject to the rising power of the Indo-Europeans; and the coming of these peoples, culminating with the appearance of Cyrus and the liberating influences which his rule was to bring to mankind, was but the realisation of the long-ordained purpose of God. The Ionians had emerged from the age of myth and tradition and were speculating on the causes of the cosmic order, the Buddha was in search of the permanent truths of life, and Zoroaster was concerned with the revelation of a god of life and goodness. But, inheriting the revealed truths of earlier Hebrew prophecy and stimulated by the intellectual ferment of his age, Deutero-Isaiah declared that the world was created by One God, eternal in His Being, universal in His sovereignty and whose message to mankind is, 'Come unto me and be ye saved all the ends of the earth.' Thus of all the developments of thought which converged to make the exilic age one of the most significant in history this conception of God as enunciated by Deutero-Isaiah has had the most profound consequences for the spiritual life of man.

INDEX

SUBJECTS

AUTHORS